How to Own Working From Home: The Pandemic Edition
©2021, Bunny Young and Chris Harris
Boss On Purpose LLC

Edited by Erin Leigh

All rights reserved.

ISBN: 978-1-950306-15-2
ISBN eBook: 978-1-950306-11-4

HOW TO OWN

WORKING FROM HOME

THE PANDEMIC EDITION

BUNNY YOUNG AND CHRIS HARRIS

TABLE OF CONTENTS

CONFESSION FROM THE EDITOR	1
PREFACE	3
WARNING: READ BEFORE YOU DIVE IN	7
CHAPTER 1: WHAT JUST HAPPENED?	9
CHAPTER 2: WHAT MATTERS MOST?	21
CHAPTER 3: YOU ARE WHERE YOU ARE	32
CHAPTER 4: FALL IN 🖤 WITH BOUNDARIES	44
CHAPTER 5: INSANE PRODUCTIVITY	55
PART 1 - REDUCE & REMOVE	59
PART 2 - HONE YOUR FOCUS	66
PART 3 - BE PRESENT	73
PART 4 - JUST FOR PARENTS	76
CHAPTER 6: THINK 🧠 LIKE A BOSS	87
CHAPTER 7: STAYING POSITIVE WHEN THINGS SUCK	98
CHAPTER 8: HOW TO MAKE A DIFFERENCE EVERY DAY (SERIOUSLY!)	110
CHAPTER 9: NOW IT'S YOUR TURN…	123
EPILOGUE (IS IT REALLY OVER?)	125
QUICK REFERENCE GUIDE	127

CONFESSION FROM THE EDITOR

When Bunny and Chris came to me and said, "We want to co-author a book!" my first thought was, "Well, mixing these larger-than-life personalities can only end one of two ways. This could turn out to be an unending maze of data and perspectives. Or, we'll figure out how to merge their awesomeness into something enormously educational and exceptionally engaging that absolutely has the power to change people's lives."

Figuring it would be an adventure either way, I placed my bets and said yes.

Now, many months later, you're reading this book. I hope you'll agree it most certainly turned out to be the latter.

It's taken some time, but we've taken an abundance of quality content and have distilled it down to some serious, drop-it-like-it's-hot lessons on life, business, and surviving remote working, especially with kids. In these pages, there's more than enough clear, actionable content to take you from zero to 60 right now.

To help you stay focused and make the most of this content, we've included specific action items (from Chris) and journal prompts (from Bunny) at the end of every chapter. These exercises are designed to help you navigate their perspectives and *apply* what you learn (so you can actually improve your remote work experience, which is the whole point).

As editor and contributor, I am most certainly biased, but I truly believe you will be a better person in all kinds of unexpected ways for reading this book. So, take a deep breath, read on, and, with every page you turn, remember to enjoy the ride (because, in our crazy, upside-down world, what other choice is there, really?).

To your next chapter,
Erin

PREFACE

Welcome to the work-from-home world. If you're one of the countless workers suddenly stranded at home when COVID-19 hit (or some other major shift led you from cubicle to kitchen table), you've already spent some time trying to adjust to your new circumstances. But effectively making such a big transition on your own is a lot to ask.

To help you, ourselves, and hopefully the world, we took our collective years of business coaching and work-from-home expertise and poured it all into this book.

As you read, you'll find that many of the recommendations and practices in these pages blur and cross the line between work and personal. That lack of separation is intentional. With so many of us working from home, work is no longer just at work. Home is not just at home. They have become, simply, *life*.

Watching your work and your life collide in front of you, especially while trying to maintain professional productivity in the face of global uncertainty, is massively disruptive. It's unsettling. It can even be scary. But for us, straddling that line between work and home is not new. As long-standing entrepreneurs, we're both intimately familiar with the chaos (and joy!) that accompanies remote working. Those challenges you're facing? We've faced them, too. We know all about the insane distractions of constant texts and emails. The crushing deadlines from coworkers and clients. And, of course, the agony of both literal and figurative headaches caused by video conferencing all day.

We also know that if you have kids, you face the additional stress of homeschooling, babysitting, and trying to make sure the house doesn't look like a tornado hit. You get to cope with the unique pain that twists your heart every time your child begs you with tears in their eyes to play make-believe horse races with them, and you must say, "Mommy (or Daddy) is working right now."

Despite the many challenges that come with remote work (even the kid-related ones), your current circumstances are truly nothing short of a gift. *Nothing* is more rewarding than *more time* with the ones you love. Working remotely can give you that.

We've been doing it for years, and we're so glad we finally get to share it with you. As a therapist-turned-entrepreneur/speaker/consultant (Bunny) and a thought leader on productivity and revenue generation (Chris), our combined experience means we bring over 40 years of entrepreneurial and business knowledge to the table, much of it gained while working remotely.

But that doesn't mean we're perfect, not by any means.

Truth is, we originally conceived this book idea in early 2016, anticipating our message would serve primarily work-from-home entrepreneurs and salespeople. But… we had other things going on. We didn't really get going with gusto until the pandemic hit, everyone was sent home, and the remote workforce revolution began.

Suddenly, we had an idea and a message relevant to a huge population. Everyone was in desperate need of the exact kind of knowledge and support we were uniquely equipped to deliver. Talk about motivation to turn an idea around fast!

Still, it's taken us a little while to bring you this book, in part because we wanted to pack it full of everything we know while still delivering it to you concisely. But despite our hatchling idea, we, too, were unprepared for the pandemic and all its ripple effects. Though we'd both been working from home for years, quarantining and remote work orders impacted us profoundly, just like everyone else.

Fortunately, we learn quickly. As soon as we got our heads back on straight, we got to work. Now, here we are, sharing everything we know to help you overcome the remote work challenges you're facing.

PREFACE

Through this book, we are confident you *will* discover how to reach new levels of remote productivity. In addition, we hope the guidance on these pages helps you become a more purposeful, productive, and positive human all around… no matter where you choose to lay your laptop.

Stay safe and stay sane,
Bunny & Chris

WARNING: READ BEFORE YOU DIVE IN

If you aren't serious about wanting to become a remote working ninja, put this book down right now. Really. Now's your chance. Just walk away, and go back to your "normal" (cough) life.

Still here? Buckle up, hold on, and let's dig in.

Six things you *must* do to get the most out of this book:

1. Reserve time each week to read and complete at least one chapter.

2. Do the exercises at the end of each chapter. They aren't there for fluff. Completing them is what takes this book from concept to reality.

3. Make sure you have a dedicated notebook or journal to use (there will be plenty of stuff to write in it, promise).

4. Resist the urge to skip around. Each chapter builds on the previous one.

5. Change is sometimes difficult, and it takes time. During this book, we are going to ask you to change *a lot* (more on that later). Your job is to show up, keep doing the work, and be patient with yourself.

6. Keep an open mind as we explore new ideas. The concepts we'll be sharing probably look, sound, and feel different than what you already know. At times, it may be tough to take it all in and process it all. That's expected. Just take a deep breath, keep going, and focus on your opportunity for growth!

CHAPTER 1:
WHAT JUST HAPPENED?

CHRIS

It was mid-August 2017, a weekday around 11 AM. I'd just completed the finishing touches on a proposal I'd been working on for over a month. It was a beast of a project, and I felt ragged and fried. My wife was headed out of town for the second weekend in a row, and it was the tenth week of my daughter being at home around the clock—no school, daycare, or camp. I was desperate for some alone time to rest my mind and recharge my batteries, but there were still more tasks on the to-do list.

Sighing to myself, I clicked open another window on my laptop and tried to mentally rouse myself to dig into another project. Spontaneously, my daughter crawled into my lap and said, "I love you, Daddy."

I stared at the screen for a moment. Without hitting another key, I closed the laptop. My choice in that moment was obvious: It was more important for me to be a good father than a productive entrepreneur.

Looking down at my daughter, I asked if she'd like to go out to lunch with Daddy. The immediate hugs, giggles, and bouncing assured me it was the right thing to do.

We hopped into the truck and started down our dusty country lane, heading to her favorite restaurant. As we rounded a curve, I glanced in the rearview mirror for a glimpse of her adorable grin. But as I refocused my eyes on the road, I slammed on the brakes.

There was an airplane in a heap on the ground right in front of me.

WHY IS THERE AN AIRPLANE CRASHED ON THE GROUND IN FRONT ME??!?

I quickly turned off the motor, told my daughter to stay in the truck, and jogged toward the wreckage. My eyes were fixed on the half-conscious pilot who was audibly moaning, collapsed over his seatbelt. But before I could get too close, I was stopped by a first responder shouting, "Get back! This area is not safe! There's a gas spill!"

My heart jumped out of my chest. In full view of the entire scene now, I noticed there were dozens of safety vehicles bearing down on this two-seater plane that had attempted an emergency landing in my neighbor's field. Unsuccessful, the plane had crashed, tearing through a wooden fence line before coming to a halt in the middle of my road, a mere 400 yards from my house.

I felt frozen. I wanted to do something, but it was too hazardous to get near the plane. How else could I help? Then I remembered my daughter. "Oh God!" I turned and sprinted back to the truck, jumped in, floored it in reverse, pulled a 180, and sped wildly back down the road to my most trusted neighbor's house. Frantically pulling my daughter out of her car seat, I banged impatiently on the neighbor's door until she answered. As quickly as possible, I asked her to watch my daughter so I could run back to the crash site.

By the time I returned, there were over 20 emergency response vehicles parked around the crash, flanking our tiny country road. Emergency rescue workers rushed back and forth, gear strewn everywhere. The sounds of sirens and walkie-talkies filled the air, along with the pungent smell of burning plastic. At the center of all of it was a mangled, single prop plane with the pilot trapped inside. It was surreal.

As I watched what appeared to be chaos, I noticed a focused calm slowly fell over the entire scene. A team of rescue workers were working in choreographed harmony to extract the injured pilot. It took almost an hour before they successfully pulled him from the torn-up cockpit, loaded him into a helicopter, and flew him to the nearest trauma center.

I later learned the pilot succumbed to his injuries and died soon after. He was just 38 years old, married, with two school-aged children.

Now, I'm just a regular human being, living in our crazy, unpredictable world. As a small business owner, I admittedly get caught up in the pressure of things like "deadlines" and "goals" and "revenue growth." I get frustrated with clients who drag their feet, trying to decide whether or not to purchase my services. Sometimes, I bite off more than I can chew, burn out, and lose sight of what matters most: my health and the health and happiness of the people I love and care about.

But there have been several times in my life when the universe has shaken me and said, "Hey, take a look around you, man! I know you've got goals and deadlines, but don't forget to appreciate what you've got *right now!*" That message has come to me in many forms over the years.

This was one of those moments: a plane fell out of the sky, and literally crashed in my backyard. I know I will never forget it.

That night, as I lay down in bed, closed my eyes, and breathed deeply, I found myself gratefully counting the many good things already in my life. Without question, what mattered most was already with me: I had a roof over my head, my wife (who had postponed her trip for a day to stay with us) sleeping soundly next to me, and a loving, wiggly five-year-old burrowed under my arm because she didn't want to be alone in her room.

Perhaps you've never had a plane crash in your backyard. But I bet you've been where I've been, standing alongside the scene of a crisis, unsure where to go, what to do, or how to help. We've all been there. In early 2020, a pandemic came crashing down seemingly out of nowhere, right into everyone's backyards. We all scrambled for an "emergency landing" as we dealt with mounting fear and uncertainty. We watched, filled with anxiety and worry, while front line workers toiled to save lives, fighting the odds.

I don't need another plane in my yard for me to recognize that the shock of COVID (and all its implications and repercussions) has been another of those "universe" moments, reminding me to focus on what is truly important.

Even in the moments when my mind recoils at the magnitude of what has happened and all that has changed, I am grateful for what I have in my life right now.

BUNNY

I like to think I have some pretty good stories, but I've never had a plane crash in my yard. In fact, I'm pretty sure none of my stories even come close to that, so I'll just let Chris' tale stand alone and be awesome.

I can tell you, though, that even without a plane crash, I've been through my fair share of traumatic events, just as you probably have. And, just like you, I've survived every time. In fact, I pride myself on my ability to stand strong in the face of challenge and uncertainty, as should you (seriously, you're stronger than you think).

However, when the virus started spreading, it took things to a whole new level. It *changed* us. Without warning, we were sent home from all our routine activities and told not to come back. Almost overnight, we morphed from "normal" business professionals into remote workers, teachers, therapists, future predictors, and pop tart hoarders. Some of us appeared to make the transition quickly, only to be taken over by emotions later on. Others reeled upfront, then eventually found their way. Some of us pivoted immediately, then again, then again, trying to find our way forward. And some of us froze in place, unsure what to do, just hoping to wait it out.

All the while, every single one of us was trying not to freak the hell out that the entire world was shutting down.

Whew. Now that we are where we are, I sometimes think about what I would say if I had the opportunity to call up my old, pre-pandemic self, circa February 2020. Maybe that chat would go something like this:

Current Bunny: Hey, listen - it may sound odd, but you are going to want to stock up on some toilet paper and buy a bunch of Zoom stock. Now.

Pre-COVID Bunny: Um, okay, but why?

Current Bunny: Also, you probably want to see about getting that old Xanax prescription renewed. It would be good to have 90 days' worth mail-ordered as soon as possible.

Pre-COVID Bunny: I (we?) haven't taken Xanax in years. Remember? We meditate, do yoga, go riding, get massages and pedicures, hit the gym, go out to eat with friends. We have this stress management and self-care stuff on lock. Don't be silly.

Current Bunny: Oh yeah, that reminds me, you also are going to want to get new riding boots. You're about to have a LOT more time for riding. Like, so much time that your horses are going to get tired of seeing you.

Pre-COVID Bunny: So I'm in for lots more anxiety, a ton more time on my hands, and a depressingly large need for toilet paper? You realize you sound insane, right?

Current Bunny: Sure. But in my world, insane is kind of… normal.

As I write this, still stuck at home per government orders, I am half-laughing and half-grieving the days when I could just hop in the car, hit the gym for a kick-ass cardio class, and go out to eat at a restaurant (and sit *indoors* without wondering which surfaces are safe to touch or how far away to sit from other people).

Remember back when this global pandemic thing started, and we were told we were in for what was expected to be just a two-week endeavor? When we thought we might just hunker down for a little while and wait, and then the world would go back to "normal?"

But nothing ever goes backwards. Even if you are reading this in the years since the great pandemic, I think you'll agree: The funny thing about life is that it's *always* shifting and changing in new ways. If you try, it's easy to find something "unprecedented" about every single moment in time. So why do we keep trying to make things "normal?" What does that even mean?

Change is always happening, and, for the most part, we handle life's little ups and downs fairly well. Sometimes, though, change takes us beyond our limits. When we experience an extremely distressing or disturbing experience, it is known as *trauma*.

Trauma can take many forms, such as:

- Finding out there's suddenly a massively contagious virus with the power to wipe out over a quarter of a million Americans (per the predictions being shared through the media when Chris and I first sat down to write this book)

- Learning you'll no longer be going in to the office and will now be working from home, even though you were completely unprepared for the change and don't know how to work from home effectively

- Getting the news that schools are sending kids home and asking them to master distance learning, which means you'll have to master distance learning, too, while also somehow trying to work productively in a new, distraction-filled environment

Trauma also takes countless non-pandemic-y forms: moving homes, getting divorced, changing jobs, losing a loved one, and even having a baby. Basically, anything that upends your normal, day-to-day routine can be traumatic.

So, if you're still feeling a little unsure about your ability to weather the current storm, take a look back at your past. I can just about guarantee that when you do, you'll easily see that your current challenge, insane or impossible as it may feel, is not the first time you have experienced a major change or shift in your life.

And, would you look at that? Whatever trauma happened in your past, *you survived*. You're here now, and that makes you a survivor. So give yourself some credit just for making it this far. (Like I said, you're stronger than you think.) Sure, maybe last time around it wasn't a global pandemic, but whatever it was, you made it through, even if you came out with a few scars. You learned, adapted, and grew. You proved you know how to survive change, even traumatic change.

That means you can survive your current transition or trauma, too.

How? Well, wherever we are, we must accept that we are there. Because everything always changes, we cannot go backwards. Neither can we rush forwards into some arbitrary "new normal" in an attempt to hold onto the remaining fragments of what used to be. Instead, we need to accept that things simply are what they are, right now.

Accepting that truth gives you space to take a deep breath, gather your wits, and look around you. With acceptance, you can start the process of getting your head around what has happened, identifying who's still with you (hint: we're right here, cheering you on), and determining what you can and will do in response to the trauma or situation.

To figure out how you want to respond to what's going on around you, first pause and acknowledge your feelings. Specifically, I'm talking about grief and loss. As humans, when dealing with trauma, we need to verbalize what's happened in our world and our lives if we want to be able to really move forward. We need to hear how others are dealing with the same kinds of challenges, to recognize we are not alone.

But it can be tough to talk about fears and worries, especially in the face of uncertainty. We question our own reactions and tend to judge ourselves by old standards, even though what we're feeling is completely legitimate and understandable.

Here's a great example: I never actually thought I could miss going to the grocery store. But when quarantine happened, I did. It wasn't that I missed the store itself so much. It was that I missed the *freedom* of my former grocery shopping experience. Before, I would just aimlessly wander the aisles to see what was there, never thinking about what I might be exposing myself to by staying for too long or worrying about who had touched which handles before me. Those thoughts never crossed my mind. I was just drifting for a moment in time.

Now that things are different, I genuinely miss the old way of grocery shopping. It sounds silly to say, right? But it's true, and it's real. If I go to the grocery store at all instead of ordering online, it's a different experience altogether. My headspace is more rigid, and I feel more anxious. My thoughts aren't flowing freely. They're focused on avoiding germs and getting in and out of there as quickly as possible.

Maybe you relate. As you contemplate all that has happened, do you find your thoughts drifting to the past, wishing for the relative ease of what used to be, both personally and professionally? Do you, like me, find yourself reflecting on your "old life" and comparing it with where you are now? If you do, does your old life seem almost foreign? Like it was a completely different world, not one you lived in every day mere months ago? It's a weird feeling, isn't it?

If this dissociative feeling sounds familiar, it's no surprise. Having been through trauma, at a psychological level what you are now processing is *loss*. Your perspective has changed, and you can't go back. Right now, compared with the ease of the past, the present feels very different and challenging. Things that once brought a sense of comfort no longer do. Even something as simple as a trip to the grocery store may trigger feelings of grief. And that's just one tiny example among kajillions. Another more powerful pandemic example is the loss of the ability to drop your kids off at school, the loss of knowing what you're doing is right and good for them, and the loss of confidence that they will be both safe and taught well. There's also the subsequent loss of concentration that comes from questioning their safety and your own and the loss of your ability to be present with coworkers and clients because of your concerns. You may even feel like you've lost your confident, committed professional identity… and the peace of mind that once came with it.

Working from home, without the familiar, structured environment of your professional office, thoughts like these can quickly start to swirl. And, because you're at home, they can interfere with your productivity *and* your personal life. The separation between work and life, blurry as it was before, is now practically nonexistent.

Before you started working from home, you at least had a commute. As much as you may have complained about the drive, as you walked out of the building, got into your car, and began the decompression process of changing over from your professional to your personal life, you experienced a form of release: the sensation of a job well done, a chapter closed, a day finished. The physical act of driving—a different headspace than working—and the time you spent doing it helped with the transition from business meetings to bedtime stories. But now, that time is gone.

In the midst of major life transition, the things we once believed steady, stable, and secure often change, sometimes incredibly quickly. In order to survive the transition, we must give ourselves time and permission to grieve the old in addition to assimilating the new.

We must also remember that grief is more than just a set of stages. It is a process. It comes and goes in waves of intensity and emotion. Grief's timing varies by person. Just like trauma itself, grief offers no predictability, no "normal." The journey is never exactly the same.

And, you never have to bear it all alone.

As you weather this storm and the inevitable storms of change to come, I invite you to become a buffalo. Unlike cows, who scatter and run away when they see a storm (and ultimately spend more time in stormy weather because they are running *with* the storm), buffalo turn and face oncoming storms directly. Shoulder to shoulder, as a herd, they purposefully walk forward, *through* the storm. Together, they ensure they all see sunnier skies.

TAKE ACTION!

Shift Your Perspective *(Chris)*

With so much going on, it's no wonder many of us currently have a constant, nagging feeling that parts of our world are spinning out of control.

Being grateful and expressing gratitude is a wonderful way to switch your mental focus and attitude. A typical gratitude journal does wonders in the *feel good* category. However, it often falls short in facilitating a lasting mindset shift. To help retrain your brain to feel more positive and grateful for what you have (and *will* have in the future), here is a little exercise.

These questions may seem a little weird, but rest assured they are intentional and in a particular order.

Every night before bed, answer these four questions:

1. Even if your day went badly, what was one small thing that went well today?

2. What was the hands-down *best* thing that happened to you today?

3. For what are you most grateful, as you are writing this right now?

4. What is the one thing you are most *excited* about *tomorrow*?

Journal It Out *(Bunny)*

This book is designed to help you increase your confidence and clarity in your entire life, not just around working remotely. To achieve that goal, in addition to completing each chapter's recommended exercise(s), it is important to give yourself space to reflect on your own reactions and insights. Capturing your thoughts, feelings, and ideas in a journal is an excellent way to document your personal growth.

You will find each chapter's journaling section has the same initial three "baseline" questions followed by a few chapter-specific questions.

Do you have to answer every single question for every chapter?

No.

Will you get more out of this book if you do the journaling portions?

Absolutely.

You'll also notice this question throughout this book (but not in every chapter):

"On a scale from 1-10, how confident are you in your ability to be productive while working remotely?"

Each time you see this question, check in with yourself, answer honestly, and compare your answer to your previous answer(s). As you make your way through this book, this periodic gauge will give you a clear way to measure your progress and improvement.

Chapter 1 Journal Questions:

What is one thought or concept you took away from this chapter?

Did any familiar themes, fears, or habits of thought come up for you as you read this chapter? Do any of these patterns have the power to limit your progress? If so, how could you alter your thinking and reframe those thoughts to keep you moving forward?

Right now I am feeling:

_____

On a scale from 1-10, how confident are you in your ability to be productive while working remotely?

Bonus non-journaling questions, just for Chapter 1:

- Did you intentionally reserve time in your calendar to read this chapter? If not, remember to do so for each chapter as you move forward with this awesome book!

- Did you join our online Boss On Purpose community yet? No? Then go to www.BossOnPurpose.com, and join us now!

CHAPTER 2:
WHAT MATTERS MOST?

CHRIS

During the calm moments of our lives, most of us don't think about our personal ethics and values. Though we all *have* core values—those inner beliefs and principles that guide our lives and choices and help us decide what's right and wrong—for the most part, we don't pay them much heed. Daily life doesn't often push us in deep, ethical ways.

But sometimes, it does, like when a literal global plague sweeps the world.

When the virus hit, our comfortable, daily rhythm was shaken. With essentials like toilet paper, cleaning supplies, and hand sanitizer suddenly hard to come by, we all had to make a choice as to how we would respond to things like scarcity, unfamiliar sources of danger, and fear.

In the midst of it all, I found myself thinking frequently of my good friend, John, who happens to be an expert in sociology and teaching theory. Specifically, I kept recalling a story John shared with me when we'd had lunch together a few months before the work-from-home orders started to rain down.

During our conversation, John had asked me how often my clients struggled to stay true to their own core values and personal code of ethics while engaged in the throes of their professional endeavors. I'd told him it was so common I'd actually developed an exercise to address the issue.

"Is your values exercise powerful enough to stand up to *the* test?" he asked.

"I'm not sure what you mean," I replied.

"In the early 90s," John shared, "I was in Special Forces training. One morning, very early, I was jarred out of my sleep along with the rest of my platoon. We were ordered to the tarmac, where we sat for countless hours, waiting to hear the words GO or NO-GO [to Iraq]. You can imagine the intensity of emotions we felt, the chaotic thoughts flying through our heads, and the nerves twisting our stomachs as we sat on our rucksacks, waiting for our orders… awaiting our fate.

"After what seemed like an eternity, a seasoned staff sergeant stood in front of us, cleared his throat, and said,

'Before we go over there, I want each of you to think about something long and hard. You have been trained well. You are going to be barraged with tough situations that will call into question your core values and your ethics. You will be repeatedly faced with decisions that will challenge your sense of right and wrong, and you might only have a split second to make crucial decisions. Right now, while you're sitting here on this tarmac, I want you to imagine all kinds of scenarios involving life and death and human suffering. As you go through these scenarios in your mind, I want you to get clear on where *you* draw the line for yourself—specifically, what actions you'd either be willing or not willing to take.

'Once you've gotten clear on that question, you are to keep the answer to yourself. Do not tell another living soul. Trust me, this will serve you down the road. Because once you're over there in the heat of the moment, facing life-and-death situations, you won't have time for soul-searching. Luckily, the question at that point won't be about where you draw the line because you've already identified that for yourself today. The question will be: Are you willing to cross that line? Are you willing to violate your own code of ethics? We are talking about what you think is right and wrong—No one else!

'So remember this: Once you make the decision to cross that line, it will be all the easier for you to cross it again… and again… and again. And, if you cross that line enough times, you will eventually lose sight of the line altogether; it will be as if that line never existed. And putting that line back in place will prove to be nearly impossible.'

"It was a pivotal moment for me," John added.

A short while after the sergeant concluded his impassioned speech, John had been given orders to stand down and was subsequently shipped back to his base. But he never forgot that unorthodox, extremely powerful message about intimately knowing his values. He took the lesson to heart, and, within a few years, he was pursuing a PhD. Based on that specific moment and lesson, John established a whole new life for himself, one with a wife, a family, and very clear, defined values.

John's story impacted me deeply, so much so that I modified my own approach to getting clear on values. Now, I go deeper. The values uncovered are more powerful. And my clients and I have John to thank for that.

To give it a try yourself, check out the exercise at the end of this chapter.

BUNNY

As an Army wife, I have the utmost respect for John and all the other amazing people who are serving and have served our country. Without them, fear and uncertainty would be far more common in our lives during non-pandemic times, too. But you definitely don't have to be Special Forces to benefit from the lessons and preparations John's sergeant encouraged him to consider. They are relevant no matter who you are or what you do.

Living in a world where tough decisions are pretty much par for the course, clearly knowing your values is essential. Knowing your values allows you to intentionally walk your own moral path when challenges arise. Those values guide your reactions and responses to everything life sends you, including contagious viruses, wearing masks, and working from home.

So, identify your values. Really get to know them. Do Chris' exercise at the end of this chapter. And, don't stop there.

Once you know your values, apply them. Use them to guide you on your path to wherever you're going. Let them help you figure out what you want and why it matters whether you get there at all.

For me, knowing *what* I want and *why* I want it is as non-negotiable as knowing my values. To stay in touch with my *what* and my *why,* I like to do an exercise where I write, "What do you want?" at the top of a page. Then, I give myself 20 minutes to brain-dump my list of answers, totally unfiltered. Each time I do it, I find this little exercise both revealing and cathartic because it serves as both a reminder and a reality check.

As I read over my unfiltered list, I always gain perspective. Seeing what I want clearly written out on paper refocuses my thoughts and mindset on my goals, not my challenges. It helps me identify how I want certain situations to work out, which often helps me see what I can do to positively influence the situation. And, maybe most importantly, on almost every "What do I want?" list I write, I find that as my timer ticks down, I eventually start listing out my much bigger, deeper "wants:" to be true to myself, to be an awesome mom and wife, to serve my clients well, and to make a difference in the world. These bigger, deeper answers are more than just *what*. They're far closer to my *why*, my soul-deep motivation for life. They're the reasons I keep showing up every day, even when times are tough.

Inevitably, as I read through these deeper items on the list, just about any challenge I am facing fades away. I don't fight to make it happen. The challenge simply pales in comparison with my *whats* and *why* they're important to me, and I find myself calm and refocused.

Every time I go through this practice, I experience this kind of positive mindset shift, especially if I've been feeling a little mentally or emotionally shaky (and whose headspace isn't shaken up these days?). Regularly writing out what I want and why helps keep me focused and positive. In other words, doing this exercise helps me keep my intentions front and center.

Why the focus on mindset and intentions? Well, neuroscience (specifically *The Science of Intention*, by Miranda Weindling) has proven that when you consciously set an intention, your subconscious mind retains awareness of that intention *even when you are not consciously thinking about it.*

So, by making a conscious choice to mentally anchor a specific goal or intention in your mind, you embed it in the subconscious, too. That means *whether you're aware of it or not, you're always focused on your goal or vision.* Over time, your repeated conscious and subconscious thoughts about that goal spark motivation, new choices, and different behaviors and actions.

This is why vision boarding and other visualization exercises can be so effective. By consistently feeding your brain your positive dreams and goals, you eventually start to see those outcomes manifest in your reality. (More to come in Chapter 7 on positive brain food and spreading good vibes intentionally.)

Sadly, especially in the professional world, but really in both personal and professional life, we rarely talk about mindset and intentions. Instead, we tend to fill our weeks with data and day-to-day metrics: P&L statements, growth goals, competitive advantage, etc. While some focus on these topics is necessary, when we're too caught up in them, we lose sight of the bigger picture, which can lead us to forget why we're really here.

I recently spoke to a friend who was so stressed about growing her company. When I asked her why she felt she had to grow, she went silent for a moment. Finally, she replied, "Well, because if you are not growing, then what is the point?"

The point is that growth simply for the sake of growth, with no true passion or motivation or *why*, is not healthy. That kind of "growth" is more like activity for the sake of movement, hanging out on the proverbial hamster wheel. The deep fulfillment most of us crave cannot come from that type of growth.

Real growth is about moving closer to your *why*. It is about making your goals and dreams a reality, not just watching profits rise on your P&L or finding ways to do, have, or become *more*.

Instead of asking, "How can I get more?" try asking yourself, "What do I really want... when I get more? How will having *more* add greater value to my life?"

Once you know what you want—and I mean *really* know, not just jumping on the bandwagon of what everyone else wants or says they want—make a point to mentally and emotionally bring that picture to life. See it clearly in your mind. Feel the deep, powerful emotions your *what* inspires. Set your intention to live in a way that takes you there. At every turn, allow your vision to guide you as you align your choices with your intention.

With me? Not quite? Let's try an example.

My business logo for A Better Place Consulting is a starfish, based on a story about a boy who made a life-changing difference to individual starfish washed up on the beach by throwing them back into the ocean one by one. When I found that story, I knew that was how I wanted to run my business: Focus fully on each individual client, be present, and make as much of an impact on that one client as possible. By making a difference for each of them—my *what*—I hoped they, in turn, would also go out and make the world a better place (thereby contributing to my *why*—my big motivation for getting out there and making it happen every day).

As my business grew, most of my client engagements aligned with this vision perfectly. My style and approach worked well for them. I knew I made a difference to each one. And I knew they were making a difference in the world, too.

Then, one day, I was referred to a different kind of client, one that could meet our company's entire quarterly financial goal with just one contract... if I served him well.

Unfortunately, during the initial meeting, as I began asking questions and discussing expectations, I discovered this client had torn through a number of consultants before me with no real progress.

This was no lone starfish stranded on the beach, longing to be returned to the surf. This was a great white shark thrashing around on the shore, attacking everyone who tried to help. If I was going to serve him, my normal approach wouldn't work.

But was taking on a client, especially one so different from my starfish clients, still aligned with my vision?

After reflecting on it, I decided I had two options. My first option was to walk away, refuse to work with him, and hope he found someone else to help him before he destroyed everything he'd built, including the company and team he was in charge of. That would also mean forgetting about the huge, positive impact he had the potential to make on the world.

Or, I could recognize he would never be a starfish and let go of my "normal" way of doing things. I could try to meet him where he was and maybe, just maybe, make a difference where no one else could, freeing him to positively impact the world.

Weighing my options carefully, I decided to help.

To make it work, I made a point to explore his mindset, *what*, and *why* with him deeply. Amazingly, not even a month into our engagement, he relaxed and stopped fighting so hard. With newfound focus, he renewed his efforts, this time in a productive way. In no time, his business had turned completely around, and he even had his ocean view, which had been a big part of his *what*, both at home and at the office. Since then, he has continued making giant waves of positive impact at every turn.

Even though he wasn't the kind of client I'd expected or imagined, serving him had been true to my *what* and *why*. With my intentions guiding me, I'd contributed to making the world a better place in a much bigger way than ever before.

So, let me ask again: What do you want?

Not others. *You*. What makes your soul happy?

If you don't know the answer yet, give it some serious time and thought. Try a "What do I want?" brain dump, like I do. See if it helps. Just make the time to ask yourself this crucial question. Doing so now will save you from waking up years down the road with the realization that you spent way too much time missing out on what really matters to you.

Once you find the answer to what you want, don't stop there, especially if what you want feels only surface-deep. If that's the case, you still need to go deeper.

To move beneath surface-level wants, take the thing you think you want, and start asking yourself *why* you want it. Ask "Why do I want that?" at least five to seven times. Every time you pose this question and answer it, you are peeling away another layer. You are bringing your dreams into greater focus and getting closer to the deep, profound truth underneath. Keep asking why, pulling back layer after layer, until your answers stop feeling surface-level and begin to resonate with your soul.

When that happens, you will have reached a soul-level truth. You will know what you want and exactly why your vision, dreams, and aspirations matter to you. You'll be ready to make a real difference in the world.

TAKE ACTION!

Know Your Values *(Chris)*

Although you might not actually be going off to war, your work, your relationships, working from home means your household can often resemble a war zone. Yes, it's stressful at times, but true core values aren't really tested unless there is a lot on the line (meaning there are real, dire consequences if you do or do not take action based on your core values). It seems clear cut, but it rarely is.

For instance, do you call the police if you see someone throw a brick through a store owner's window? Does that change if you are going on a beach trip with your family when you witness the event while pumping gas… and you are already running four hours late? Does it change if the store owner is a good friend of yours?

Knowing your values is the first step in answering these questions truthfully. Here's how.

1. Find a quiet window of time when you are not distracted, and take the opportunity to reflect on what is deeply important to you (your values).

2. Write down the answers to the following questions:

    a. Who do I want to become in the next three years?

    b. What *values* are foundational to that version of myself?

    c. How will I demonstrate those values?

    Write your answers in the present tense, as if you are already living that future right now.

Examples: I make time for my son. I show my neighbor kindness every day. I am patient with my coworkers. I give 100% effort on my work.

4. Within each answer, circle the key word(s) that represents the value in each action statement.
   Examples: make time, show kindness every day, I am patient, 100%effort

5. Consider your reactions to your current environment (physical, emotional, mental, social). In what ways are the circled values from the previous question already being tested?

6. Now that they are clearly identified, what could you do differently to strengthen and embody these values?

The Power of Purpose *(Bunny)*

The filter through which we view our lives greatly impacts how we feel about our progress or achievements. Many people automatically filter their lives according to what others have taught them, but we all have the power to choose our filters intentionally.

In order to create and live the life I desire, I choose to filter my life through *my purpose*. Your purpose can guide and direct you, too, once you know it clearly.

To check in with yourself, clearly define your purpose, and ensure your current activities are aligned with your bigger picture and life goals:

1. Dedicate 45 minutes to go through this "Power of Purpose" exercise.

2. During your allotted time, set a timer for 20 minutes, and write "What do I want?" at the top of a page. Brain dump your answers.

3. Once your timer goes off, for each item on your list, ask yourself, "Why do I want that?" Keep asking why five to seven times for each item, until you reach a soul-deep answer. Write down this deeper why for each item.

4. Now consider your "real whys" list, and view it through the lens of your values. Which of the things you want and your deep whys align most clearly with the values you identified in Chris' exercise above?

   Chances are, the answers or areas where you see the greatest alignment among *what, why,* and your values are closest to your true purpose.

5. If you do NOT see alignment among your *what, why,* and values, the next step is to figure out the disconnect. Ask yourself, "What can I change (that is within my control) that will help me align what I want, why I want it, and my core values?"

When *what* you want and *why* you want it are aligned with your values, you have discovered your *purpose*. With this clarity, you can begin filtering your choices and actions through a new lens, one that is deeply true to you. I guarantee your life will improve as a result.

Journal It Out *(Bunny)*

What is one thought or concept you took away from this chapter?

Did any familiar themes, fears, or habits of thought come up for you as you read this chapter? Do any of these patterns have the power to limit your progress? If so, how could you alter your thinking and reframe those thoughts to keep you moving forward?

Right now I am feeling:

_____

CHAPTER 3:
YOU ARE WHERE YOU ARE

CHRIS

A few years ago, I was slated to meet with an amazing person named Linda Nash at a coffee shop in Richmond, Virginia. Regarded as one of the best business consultants in the city, she was an excellent addition to my networking circle, and she'd graciously carved out some time in her busy schedule for a face-to-face meeting with me. But rather than feeling excited about the encounter, I found myself frantic and anxious before I even sat down with her.

I've struggled with ADHD most of my life. It's challenging for me to *not* to get distracted by simple, fleeting occurrences of everyday life, such as the familiar face of a neighbor passing by my window, the flat screen broadcasting sports behind the barista, the sound of a two-year-old boy giggling and playing patty-cake with his mother on the other side of a room. These kinds of things create a collage of alluring distractions, and it's an ongoing battle for me to (try to) ignore them.

On the day of my meeting with Linda, in addition to the constant distractions of my immediate environment, I'd also had several emotional encounters. I'd started my day by checking the news, where I'd read a disturbing article about a mother of two young children who'd gone missing near my hometown. My head was still reeling from that report when I got into a heated argument with my daughter about the inappropriateness of her wearing light canvas shoes on a bitterly cold day, which resulted in a full-blown temper tantrum (on her part… though I was close!). Next up was a tense discussion with my wife regarding the never-ending list of house renovations in need of completion. All these things in quick succession left me in an agitated state as I exited my house and headed off to meet with Linda. I'd taken in an excessive amount of stimulation, it was all pulling my attention in a million directions, and my brain was completely overloaded.

When I finally arrived at the coffee shop (five minutes late, thanks to getting stuck in rush hour traffic—remember what that was like?), I was still ruminating about my stressful morning, which now included being flipped off by some guy as I pulled into the parking lot. By the time I was sitting across from Linda, the swirling mess of events and the replaying of contentious dialogue in my mind was causing a loud, distracting hum in my head, and I found it impossible to focus.

I couldn't maintain eye contact. I had difficulty following her conversation. And I repeated myself... *repeatedly!* There was no question about it: My lack of attentiveness was *visible* to her. At one point, I even got distracted with the idea of picking up my daughter from school, and caught myself glancing at the clock on my phone while Linda was talking to me.

Considering my profession as a coach means I am essentially paid to provide people with my undivided attention, it's hard to imagine my inability to pull myself together, especially in light of this golden opportunity to network with a local business mogul. But that was exactly the case. I was lost in a mental fog, and I couldn't manage to snap myself out of it.

However, to my amazement, something transpired during that meeting that changed everything.

In spite of the fact that I was obviously distracted and pretty much wasting her time, Linda remained fully poised and engaged, and gracious, giving me her undivided attention. She leaned in and asked me what I did for a living. Even as I rambled, she remained intent on absorbing my every word, all of which helped me relax, and I began relating to her more as a friendly associate, not some high-rollin' tycoon I needed to impress. I shared a few tidbits of the madness I'd experienced at home before I left for the meeting and joked about the guy who flipped me off in the parking lot, and she laughed. Never once did she break eye contact with me, even when a server dropped a plate right behind her. And when a friend recognized her and began walking toward us, she politely let him know she'd be happy to speak with him when she was done with our meeting.

For the first time in a long time, I had the privilege of feeling *fully seen, listened to, heard, and respected*. Linda's commitment to making the most of this meeting and to being present in our conversation quieted my mind. I went from utterly distracted to clear-headed, readily able to formulate my questions and answers as I connected with her. Without even trying, I slowed way down and zeroed in on the topics at hand. Simply through her attentiveness and genuine interest, she gave me the feeling that nothing else in the world mattered to her but our connection, and it ended up being a truly enjoyable and fruitful exchange.

In short, Linda saved the day.

As a highly intelligent, successful businesswoman, I have no doubt Linda knew that day that she was in the presence of someone who was off his game. But rather than let the whole thing fizzle out, she chose to make the most of the circumstances and optimize her own time, simply by hanging in there with me and offering me 100% of her attention, which never waned or wavered. In doing so, she demonstrated her commitment and enormous compassion. She proved beyond a shadow of a doubt she was worthy of the praise she so often received.

As for *presence*, that's what it all boils down to. Linda was fully committed to the time she'd carved out for this meeting, and she was intentional with her every action. She was even graceful in the way she handled her friend who'd momentarily interrupted us, demonstrating a brilliant template of highly developed empathy and communication skills that served the entire situation for *all* concerned.

Everyone in this story *won*.

Now, before you tell me, "Chris, this is a nice story, but we're not really hanging out in coffee shops the way we used to, you know," don't worry. I'm already with you. Would it have looked *exactly* the same had we been meeting remotely? Probably not. But regardless of where you work, you can still be present, gracious, kind, committed, and compassionate, and it was those particular qualities that Linda brought to our conversation that changed me.

I can't help but think that if we all give our remote coworkers and clients the same gift of presence Linda gave me, then, maybe, just maybe, this new, virtual era can be one of genuine attention and intention.

BUNNY

I'm glad Linda was there with you in that moment, Chris, and able to help ground you. We've all had moments in life where a Linda is just what we need.

That's especially true when we're facing a new world, one with the power to unexpectedly overwhelm us with feelings of helplessness and hopelessness. Uncertainty, combined with grief and loss, can put us in a pretty dark place. Which, I'll admit, is where I spent a fair amount of time in the initial wake of the pandemic. I was just trying to cope with everything that was happening, and it was a lot. It really took me down for a minute.

Maybe you were there, too. Maybe you still are. If so, that's okay. I see you, and I get it.

As someone with a health condition that puts me in the "high risk" category for catching viruses, a mom of two under the age of 10, and the owner of multiple businesses that, until early 2020, revolved largely around air travel, I was *totally* thrown off when COVID hit (and I pride myself on my self-care!). Almost overnight, everything felt unsafe. I quarantined our family immediately, locking us away from anyone who might possibly have been exposed.

But not everyone in our household had the same concerns I did. Partway into lockdown, my husband allowed our older daughter to go play in the neighbors front yard, in close proximity to people who were *not* locked down or taking the same precautions we were.

I just about lost it.

How could he!? Did he not see the implications? Did he want to be the one to tell our daughter she couldn't get within six feet of Mom for the next two weeks, just in case she'd been exposed? Was he willing to tell her she couldn't hug her own mother!?

Long story short, we're still married, and my daughter did not unknowingly bring the virus into our house. We were tested, and we were fine. But that moment of panic seriously rocked me. I felt so incredibly *alone* with my worries and fears.

It didn't help that my businesses were basically tanking at the same time as this whole debacle was going down at our house. When we were all ordered to stay home, over the span of just three days, my company lost over a quarter of a million dollars worth of contracts. I'd planned on 2020 being a heavy year of speaking for me, but conferences were suddenly canceled, and speakers were no longer needed. Clients who feared a plummeting stock market cut back on their team development spending. Individual coaching clients no longer felt certain they could afford the investment of working with our coaches because their clients were pulling back on spending, too. And traveling to any of these locations to offer on-site support was out of the question for so many reasons.

Fortunately, for insane situations like these (as well as other, somewhat less insane business situations), I have mentors and a mastermind group. Knowing I needed help and some perspective, I decided to share this 72-hour nightmare. Their reactions were both encouraging and surprising. The resounding response was, "It may seem bad, but you've been through a recession before. You can definitely figure something out."

More than once, a mentor has also reminded me, "Is someone paying you to complain and beat yourself up? If not, get back to activities that actually move your business forward!" Point taken.

So, in the face of what felt like doom, I rallied. I brainstormed. I got focused, and I realigned myself with my purpose. As I did, I remembered (how could I forget?! I'm calling it "pandemic brain") that I had an amazing team of Linda-esque resources already in my corner in the form of my team. We'd been through so many challenges together, and we'd proven our ability to survive and overcome them all. I knew we would make it through this, too.

Head back in the game, I began using the same strategies I recommended to my clients in my own business and life immediately. Now you can, too.

1. Embrace the Virtual World (It's Not Going Anywhere)

Rather than flying out to my clients' locations to speak onsite or conduct live workshops, I began sending my clients and their newly remote teams pre-recorded video content. This approach kept me off planes and out of airports, but providing virtual access to our coaching and consulting videos also gave our clients and their teams a way to learn from wherever they happen to be physically working.

While you may not be creating video content for teams like I am, you can still embrace virtual connection. Yes, I know you're probably Zoomed out already, but virtual meetings really are a huge benefit to the remote working world. Since we became business partners back in 2016, Chris has relentlessly harassed me about "still" doing in-person meetings. (He has done almost all of his client meetings virtually for many, many years, so when companies left and right started encouraging remote work to prevent the spread of COVID, he could not wait to call me with a big, ol' "I told you so.")

As much as I hate to admit it (seriously, it's painful), he isn't wrong. The ease, flexibility, and security of using technology to connect virtually when in-person connection isn't an option is genius. It's also scalable, enabling everything from one-on-one meetings to massive conferences. And, as an added bonus, virtual meetings mean you can record your discussions, retaining important details and giving those who may have missed the meeting a chance to catch up.

You can even enhance your personal connections virtually. Why not make a point to connect regularly by video call with friends and family who live farther away? Or make new friends who share similar interests? Going virtual means we're no longer restricted to our geographic communities; finding an interest-based online community can provide a new kind of fulfillment.

2. Invest Intentionally

Even though my company was a victim of this tactic, I'm sharing it because the logic still stands: Pandemic or not, proactively tightening up your budget and reexamining your spending means you keep more money in your reserves to cover any possible upcoming cash flow issues.

Let's be clear: I am in no way suggesting businesses should make massive cuts in the face of uncertainty, especially to personnel. But rethinking the professional costs of travel, live events, less-effective marketing tactics, and other such expenditures can help create a reserve of money for company overhead, which is pretty nice to have for a rainy day (or a pandemic-y day, or whatever).

Though your personal investments will of course look different than the costs of doing business, having a personal reserve of money to help cover your costs of living during times of uncertainty is also a great idea. Why not make now the time to reconsider where and how you're directing your dollars?

A great way to start is to ask yourself, "Which of my/our expenses are absolutely necessary?" List out what you deeply feel must stay Then, before adding anything else to your list, reconsider each further expense you currently have. Why do you invest in it? What does it do for you? How does it improve your life? Is there a way to accomplish the same outcome in another creative, more affordable way? Can you afford to suspend that expense temporarily?

Here's an example of shifting investments in the face of uncertainty. When COVID hit, our company temporarily made the choice to cut back on social media ads that point to our work-life alignment programs. It was quite clear no one was thinking about investing in their long-term happiness in that moment. Everyone's main focus was buying hand sanitizer (obviously) and copious amounts of toilet paper (why?). Instead of continuing to invest in social media, we stopped putting dollars into ads and started putting heads together. Intentionally, we took the cash we saved and set it aside to help cover our overhead.

With new focus, we did a little pivoting and came up with our "Mental Wellness in the Workplace" program. This new, timely program was the perfect chance to relaunch our social media ads, which we did with great success. We discovered that pausing our spending on our "regularly scheduled programming" had given us the space and motivation to create an even better solution to share with the world, and, as our ads started rolling, it turned out to be our best performing ad campaign ever!

3. Decrease Stress

Though stress may not be top of mind, it's even sneakier than COVID—and it could increase your chances of catching it.

How? When you are under significant stress, your immunity and ability to fight off disease decreases. So, ironic as it seems, feeling anxious about the unknown impacts of coronavirus might actually increase your risk for COVID as well as every other virus and bug out there.

To help take the edge off and counteract some of that tension and anxiety, I strongly recommend upping your self-care. I'm not saying you need to head out on a week-long yoga retreat tomorrow (although a yoga video isn't a bad idea). Just make a point to squeeze in some "you time" as often as possible. Since it's almost impossible to do "too much" meditation or practice an overabundance of mindfulness, adopt a "more is better" mentality. It's one of the few times in life where less isn't more; more is more. Self-care decreases stress *and* boosts immunity.

4. Reach Out (to Clients, Connections, Friends, Whomever!)

Of all the strategies on my list of "things I can control in the face of uncontrollable things," I love this one the most.

Remember, we are all human beings first and foremost, and our need for connection is tribal and natural. Suddenly working from home, whether by choice or in the name of health and safety, is going to get lonely. When you're feeling all alone, simply hearing from a valued connection, fellow business owner, coach, mentor, or dear friend can be a huge gift. Even if it's just calling to say, "Hey, how are you? I am a little unsure, too, but here is some stuff I am planning on doing," it makes a big difference knowing there is still someone out there who cares.

Reaching out—with the genuine intention of connecting, relating, and providing reassurance, not selling!—*is* doing the work. Intentionally connecting in the face of uncertainty… Showing up authentically with a desire to serve… Being present… These things are completely aligned with our company's values and our vision. Why not use current circumstances as an excuse to demonstrate them?

As an unexpected bonus, the honest and humble conversations we've had with our clients and connections as a result of reaching out have also given our team tremendous insight into how we can move forward. Their heartfelt responses revealed common themes, problems we could actually help solve. With their input, we stretched and grew, and, as we did, our relationships with them grew stronger. They felt like we were creating something special for them and with them (which was true!), and, because these new services and tools were designed to address their unique obstacles and challenges, were eager to implement them.

It's true: Things are still uncertain. For all we know, they may stay that way. But we can't sit paralyzed while life passes us by. The world may look different every day, but the present is still happening right now.

It takes time for anything new to establish roots, grow, and succeed. The sooner you can accept where we are, start the journey, and begin cultivating a new way forward, the sooner you will see growth and be able to reap the fruits of your labor.

As my favorite Chinese Proverb states, "The best time to plant a tree was 20 years ago. The second best time is now." Admittedly, there are a lot of things in life over which we have very little control. But no matter what tomorrow holds, you can still take intentional action today.

TAKE ACTION!

Curb Distractions with the *WILSSN Method* (Chris)

When you're about to head into a meeting, and your mind is racing with all kinds of thoughts, it's practically impossible to focus. To bring you back to the present, especially if something is *really* distracting you, try the W.I.L.S.S.N. ("Wilson") method five minutes before your meeting.

1. **Write**

    Take out a clean sheet of paper, or open up your note app on your phone. Write out the name of what is gnawing at you. The thought here is to symbolically leave that emotional stress behind you on the page, at least temporarily, so you can be totally focused on what's in front of you.

    Example: Maybe you were in a heated exchange with your significant other over breakfast. Perhaps your car had a flat and made you late. Maybe you were notified you have a massively overdue bill. Or you may have just received an email from your irate boss. Whatever it is, write it down. Then symbolically fold the piece of paper up and put in your desk, or glove box, or seat or wherever you can literally leave it before your meeting. (If you are doing using your phone or an app, put it in a folder marked, "Stuff I can get to later.")

2. **Identify**

    Put your finger on exactly what you can control about this meeting: your attitude, your responses to questions, how you follow up, etc. Also identify what you cannot control: their attitude, whether they like or dislike what you have to say, what's going on in their life, etc.

3. **Listen**

   Close your eyes, and, for 120 seconds, just listen. Start by identifying every sound in your immediate surroundings. The hum of the lights. The air moving past the vent in the floor. The sound of your own breath and heartbeat. Then push that envelope a little further. What can you hear outside your room? A bird just outside? The fridge coming on? What about even further? A faint barking dog? Road noise, maye a jet flying high above? Tuning in to your sense of sound will pull you into the moment and dial up your ability to "hear" and "listen."

4. **See**

   Next, open your eyes and notice in extreme detail the first thing you see. If it's a desk, look closely at how glossy it is. How does the grain of the wood run? If it's the wall, can you see the individual paint strokes? The point is to really look for details. Get your eyes ready to pay attention to a singular object. This exercise will help bring you back to the present.

5. **Smile**

   Think of something that really makes you smile—because you can't be in a bad mood or worried if you are smiling! Besides, if you are on a Zoom session, nothing helps set the tone like seeing a huge, genuine smile.

6. **Now... Breathe**

   Finally, right before you start your interaction, take a deep breath in through your nose, then release it slowly out your mouth. Then, begin speaking to whomever you are meeting.

This short, simple practice will center your brain and your mood. It will also jack up the two senses which are most important during virtual meetings: listening and watching.

Journal It Out *(Bunny)*

What is one thought or concept you took away from this chapter?

Did any familiar themes, fears, or habits of thought come up for you as you read this chapter? Do any of these patterns have the power to limit your progress? If so, how could you alter your thinking and reframe those thoughts to keep you moving forward?

Right now I am feeling:

_____

Write down at least one opportunity this week where it makes sense to try Chris' W.I.L.S.S.N. exercise.

CHAPTER 4:
FALL IN 🤍 WITH BOUNDARIES

BUNNY

I'm taking the lead on this one, Chris. It's close to my heart.

It was 9 AM on Christmas morning when my phone rang. It was my boss. I knew she had been struggling with her team as well as financially and had been working overtime. So when she called, I answered.

As soon as I answered, she told me she was calling me because I have a bit of computer savviness, and she could not access the computer system at the office. She explained the problem and pleaded for my help.

But I knew my computer skills weren't the real reason she was calling. Out of all the people in the company, there were countless others with better IT skills. She'd called *me* because I had always answered her calls, and, as soon as I understood there was an issue, I had always attempted to find and implement a solution.

That was exactly why I was fielding a work call at 9 AM on Christmas. My boss knew her target, and her request hit me in my weak spot: my penchant for solving people's issues.

So, on Christmas Day, I left my kids at home with their gifts and drove out to the office, over 90 minutes away, to go and fix a computer system I had no business fixing.

Fortunately, I know better now. This incident happened before I realized my true talent lies in holding space for others to solve and address their own issues, not swooping in to do it for them. In fact, that Christmas Day call and the subsequent three-and-a-half hour round trip drive was a significant turning point for me.

As I drove, I realized I had allowed this situation to develop by always responding to my boss' cries for help. The real problem wasn't that she had called me, or that it was Christmas Day. The real problem was that *I had answered.*

Answering calls on Christmas Day was certainly not part of my job description, nor was it something I had previously agreed to doing. I knew my boss would never have called most of my coworkers on Christmas morning. But she'd called *me.* Why me? Because I had always responded to her, even outside business hours, without complaint or objection. Because, literally every time she'd called, I'd sent the message that it was okay for her to do so by answering. Because I had never set boundaries, even on Christmas morning.

I'd gotten myself into this mess.

It was a cold, hard truth to swallow.

And, I knew what I needed to do. It was time to start setting boundaries

(I also knew that if I still wanted my job, I'd need to tread carefully. "Laying down the law" about when I would and wouldn't answer calls would give the wrong message. Instead, I had to communicate my preferred availability appropriately, being sure to own my role in the scenario, too.)

Lucky for me, I had some resources at my disposal. While studying to become a therapist, we'd spent hours upon hours exploring the definition of boundaries, what it meant to set them, and how they impacted relationships and success. We also reviewed how to establish and maintain them in a healthy way. By the time I graduated with my master's degree, I had studied pretty much every aspect and therapeutic application of boundaries.

All I needed to do was actually *apply* this knowledge.

Just in case you didn't spend years studying these things, here's a quick summary on boundaries: At its simplest, a boundary is a *communicated* expectation, in the form of a verbal or written contract or agreement, that should not be violated by any of the parties involved.

Think about boundaries in the context of an employee newly hired by a company. When we get hired by a company to do a job, we (theoretically) go through a lengthy learning curve where we gain clarity around the boundaries of our job, the company's beliefs and core values, and the expectations regarding communication, dress code, professional conduct, sexual harassment, and so on.

Unfortunately, many companies never get to the part where they ask their new hires to share their personal boundaries. Instead, discussions around personal boundaries are most often ignored completely. At best, they're left up to the department head. At worst, individual employees are responsible for speaking up for themselves (a skill many of us were never taught and aren't great at). It's a rough road to navigate alone. Asking individual teammates to figure out how to establish effective, appropriate personal boundaries in the workplace is asking a lot.

Think about how much of a difference it would make to individual and team performance, team member satisfaction, and company loyalty if businesses intentionally initiated onboarding discussions to cover topics like how much we're comfortable sharing about ourselves and our family, whether we're okay responding to email after hours, what we feel are our own personal core values, and what drives us and motivates us to perform at a higher level. We'd all feel engaged and supported.

Though it is certainly possible (with the right tools and guidance) to do so in a way that supports strong work relationships between coworkers, bosses, and teammates, most of us never have conversations about clear boundaries at work. Instead, we spend all our time "on the clock," jumping when others call, feeling like we have no choice, and, over time, growing resentful or angry.

Without appropriate work boundaries, we also tend to spend more time than we should working longer, later hours, trying to make up the time we've lost to the demands of others. That's especially true working from home. It's way too easy to still be "at the office" at 10 PM (or later) when you don't have a clear boundary between work time and personal time, you know there's so much more to do, and your computer is *right there...*

But sacrificing sleep isn't the answer. Boundaries are. As you may already be experiencing, life without boundaries is tiring and draining. To truly achieve work-life alignment, especially as we explore this new, virtual work world, we must learn to set healthy boundaries, ideally as soon as possible.

Fortunately, examples of healthy boundaries are all around us. Think about state lines, country lines, operating hours, even the pandemic signs in front of stores stating masks are required for entry. They show us, in a clear and structured way, what is expected and what is acceptable in certain circumstances. Creating healthy boundaries for yourself will do the same. (Just remember to take into account the person with whom you're discussing boundaries before diving in headfirst—discussing boundaries with your boss, for example, will probably look very different than setting boundaries with your kids or your partner.)

As you start to set boundaries to reclaim your time, energy, and value, it will become clear that certain people and activities drain you. Pay attention when this happens, and consider what value these draining activities add to your life. Are they necessary to move you towards your goals? If so, continue holding space for your values as you explore these situations. Try inviting your colleagues and connections to engage with you at a different time or in a different way, one that feels more beneficial to both of you.

Today, I guarantee none of my current clients or connections would call me on Christmas Day, Christmas Eve, or even after hours on a weekday. None of them would ever think about asking anything of me on Christmas because they know family is a strong boundary for me, one I hold very dear. My girls and my husband will always come before my clients, and I will never, ever allow myself to feel guilty for putting them first.

These days, when my clients experience emergencies, my expectations are clear. I will gladly hold space virtually for them, but beyond that, I expect them to use the tools and conversations from our coaching calls to find their own solutions. I may not always be able to be there for them, but by empowering my clients to solve problems on their own, I guarantee their ability to make the world a better place, with or without me.

CHRIS

I totally agree—boundaries are essential for maintaining the kind of lifestyle you want. They're like the support beams that hold the structure of work and life, clearly creating space for serving clients, achieving goals, seeing results, and, of course, *living*.

I also like boundaries for their very practical use: They help me get things done faster and better. Since I coach, consult, and train on productivity and time management strategies, I am always searching for new ways to gain more focus and be effective with my time. As I tell my clients, boundaries are an excellent way to do that, so much so that I consider them an essential tool in my productivity toolbox.

Every once in a while, I'll come across a technique that really catches my attention, usually because the concept is ridiculously simple and therefore proves wildly effective for me almost immediately. (Bonus points if it comes in the form of a memorable phrase and positively impacts multiple other facets of your life.)

I came upon one such concept in a book called *Procrastinate On Purpose*, written by Rory Vaden. About midway through the book, he stresses the importance of *holding your time sacred*. This phrase stuck with me, and I believe it's especially true today.

As Bunny alluded above, with so many of us working from home where work is only an arm's length away, there seems to be an expectation (sometimes self-imposed, sometimes imposed by others) to be available 24/7. It's tempting, too, because extra availability can feel like a guaranteed way to gain more customers, appease your boss, and give you more time to get your work done.

However, there is a nasty side effect to ongoing availability, which is summed up by Vaden in one phrase: "Every time you say 'yes' to something, you are simultaneously saying 'no' to something else."

In the context of work-life alignment, that means if you are always saying, "Yes, I'm available for work," you are also always saying, "No, I'm not available for life outside of work."

Every "yes" that comes out of your mouth or through your keyboard is a commitment, a boundary that states you will do a certain thing for someone, often at a certain time. With every "yes," you give away a little of your time and energy. And our time and energy aren't limitless, as much as many of us would like to believe.

To illustrate this idea, here are few scenarios in which saying yes to a request for your time results in an unintended (or unforeseen) broken expectation:

- In an attempt to be a good teammate, you say "yes" to helping a coworker in the afternoon so he can submit his budget numbers on time. As a result, you've said "no" to the time you'd intended to spend researching a chief competitor's new product.

- You say "yes" to taking on an additional project that promises to generate more revenue for the company in a relatively short amount of time. In doing so, you forfeit the time you'd set allotted to the new fitness program you'd promised yourself you'd begin on Monday. Your commitment to get in shape is subsequently devoured for yet another month.

- A client requests a last-minute meeting at 7 PM. You say "yes," thinking it could generate a lot of future business. As a result, you say "no" to tucking your child into bed. There's no way you'll be done by 8 PM.

Note: If you are looking for specific advice with how you can juggle work and your kiddos during crazy times, there's more for you in Chapter 5.

Saying "yes" at the right times can land awesome career opportunities, new learning experiences, and new clients. Just remember you have to be *available* in order to say yes, and if you've said yes too many times before, you will not be available when opportunity comes knocking.

Also, the more you say "yes," the more you will develop a reputation of always being available (like what happened with Bunny and her boss). In some instances this may be a good thing, but being widely available might also send a message out into the world that you've got too much time on your hands.

Most importantly, ask yourself, "Is saying 'yes' too often causing me to lose control or feel like my time isn't my own?" Is your too-tightly-scheduled or over-committed life keeping you from devoting precious time to the things that truly matter to you?

If the answer to either question is yes, it might be time to start saying "no" to a few things, too. But if you're in the habit of saying "yes," saying "no" can be tough, especially when you're feeling the expectations of others. It's not always easy to know which path to take… but more on that at the end of this chapter.

When I speak for groups, I often talk about the concept of "blocking time," which has to do with reserving specific times in advance for designated tasks such as making sales calls, meeting with clients, having a planning session, designing graphics, working on accounting, etc. To illustrate the idea of time blocking, I whip out giant Lego blocks, using different colors to represent different kinds of activities in a typical day. For example, red represents phone calls, blue represents accounting, green represents marketing meetings, and so on.

In these talks, everyone is totally with me until I pull out the orange block, which represents personal time.

Over the years, I've discovered most people have no issues with time blocking, with one glaring exception: personal time. Personal time is quickly and easily given up in favor of doing things we perceive will be more productive or because we feel someone else needs that time more than we do. Of all our blocks, though, that orange block is the most important one. Like Rory Vaden says, our time should be held sacred, and, as the time we need and deserve to rest, relax, and recharge, personal time is no exception. In fact, it should be more like the rule. Ideally, that orange block is the cornerstone off which everything else is built.

Boundaries are what make orange time possible.

This past weekend, I was sitting on the couch with my wife (also a small business owner), watching an awesome movie. She was checking something on her computer during the commercials. Every time she got up, it took her a little longer for her to leave her laptop and to reengage with the movie.

I gently asked, "That person you're emailing? Do they want some popcorn, too?" She got the subtle hint and sheepishly snapped the laptop shut.

I patted her leg, gave her a big smile, and filled her wine glass up to the brim. She took a long sip and exclaimed, "I just wanted to knock that one email out, but I guess it can wait until tomorrow." Though her heart was in the right place, the problem was obvious: Work and personal life were intermingling, and she wasn't able to focus on either.

She needed a boundary.

Laptop shut and wine in hand, we enjoyed the rest of our movie together immensely.

TAKE ACTION!

Should I "Yes," or Should I "No?" *(Chris)*

Not sure whether to say "yes" or "no" to a specific opportunity or task? Ask yourself these four questions to evaluate the specific opportunity at hand:

1. If I say yes to this action right now, will it help me gain substantially more time down the road?

2. What is the absolute worst thing that can happen if I say no to this proposition—at least for the time being?

3. How can saying "no" to this help me accomplish what I set out to finish today?

4. If I say yes, what other important things might I be saying no to?

Every time I use these questions, it helps me uncover potential blind spots, especially if I suspect I've been saying yes a little too often. They help remind me of my boundaries and the value of my energy and time. So, whatever your motivation might be for saying yes to various prospects and propositions (opportunity, obligation, helping someone in need, fear of pissing someone off, or even out of habit), remember to pause and assess the ripple effect your decision will have on your productivity and your life.

Bonus: If saying no is truly difficult for you, start with something easy. For example, set a goal to deliberately say "no" to three easy things tomorrow. It could be saying no to the dog, or saying no to eating one more brownie, or perhaps even trying saying no to cleaning up your roommate's spoon they left in the sink. Don't forget, when other people are involved, it's possible to be positive and helpful when saying "no." Try stating, "I'm not available; however, I can recommend someone who can help instead." Once you have a few easy no's under your belt, it will get easier to say no in more difficult situations.

Get Yourself Some Orange *(Chris)*

Need to incorporate a little more personal time into your schedule? Here are four simple ways to create more orange time in your daily life.

1. **Determine your "Stop Working" time.**

    No email or work-related phone calls after a designated time every day. Be consistent! (This is especially important for business owner types who have a hard time "turning it off" in the evenings and on weekends.)

2. **Schedule "Just Me" time.**

    Read a good book (not work-related), do some gardening, take a long walk, or just sit on your deck and enjoy a glass of wine. As needed, enlist the help of the people around you—ask your main squeeze or a trusted friend to watch the kids for 30 minutes (or longer) so you can enjoy time by yourself without interruption.

3. **Incorporate "Unplugged" time.**

    No TV, smartphones, or laptops! This is all about unplugging from the world for a while and slowing down.

4. **Try some "Reconnect" time.**

    Call a friend or relative with whom you haven't spoken in a long time, go on a date with your significant other, take your kids on a hike in the woods, or invite a good friend over for movie night. You can even have a dance party! Why not? The important thing here is that you spend some quality time with people you truly care about telling stories, laughing, and sharing your deeper thoughts. Just steer clear of work-related topics, and simply enjoy the pleasure of their company.

Journal It Out *(Bunny)*

What is one thought or concept you took away from this chapter?

Did any familiar themes, fears, or habits of thought come up for you as you read this chapter? Do any of these patterns have the power to limit your progress? If so, how could you alter your thinking and reframe those thoughts to keep you moving forward?

Right now I am feeling:
_____

Where do you need to say "no" in your life personally? Professionally?

In which of the above ways will you add more orange time in your life?

CHAPTER 5:
INSANE PRODUCTIVITY

CHRIS

Are you new to working from home? If you are, take it from one who's been doing it for a while: Remote work offers tremendous advantages, but it also comes with its fair share of hurdles—like plummeting productivity.

The problem is remote work forces us to address both personal and professional needs from within the same space, and that's inherently tough. As we discussed in the last chapter, setting boundaries is the first step. Boundaries allow you to create space for yourself to think, feel, work, and breathe. But once boundaries are in place, then what? Once you've carved out a few precious moments, how can you ensure you actually get things done during that time, especially from home, where distractions reign?

It was a question I asked myself way back in 2004, when I first began splitting my time between home and the office. But it wasn't until 2012, when I decided to work exclusively from home while raising our child, that I really got serious about making every second count.

During this journey, I've written countless articles, authored a few e-books, been interviewed numerous times for newspapers and podcasts, and conducted a slew of webinars and classes, all around the topics of productivity and business development. What you'll find in this chapter is a compilation of my most potent tips, hacks, and productivity strategies.

I won't lie: Some of these productivity tactics are fairly involved and will take a while to implement. Others are fairly straightforward and can be applied right away. Regardless of which you choose to use, all of them will help you get more done, in less time, while working remotely... *as long as you are committed to making some changes in your life.* (Because doing the same thing over and over and expecting different results is insanity, right? And nobody needs more of *that* in their life.)

Productive is typically defined as having the quality or power of producing, especially in abundance (such as a productive corn field). A *productive person* is someone who effectively brings about and yields results, benefits, or earnings.

These definitions are accurate, and they offer some insight, but they don't quite capture the true essence of productivity, at least not for me. My definition of a productive person is an individual who has a good track record of getting a lot of relevant, useful, and meaningful (i.e. valuable) stuff done in a timely manner... without losing their mind.

I include that extra bit at the end because there is *nothing* in the textbook definition of productivity that describes *how* one can be productive without pissing people off and/or misplacing one's soul in the quest to get it all done in the shortest amount of time. Nor is there even a glimmer of acknowledgment regarding how being productive becomes exponentially more difficult in an environment rife with distractions (every work-from-home household).

If you really want to become more productive, and you're willing to make some changes to get there, take out a piece of paper right now, and answer this incredibly important question:

What is the most important reason you want to be more productive?

(Usually we hold homework for the end of each section, but this step is so essential, it needs to happen now, before we go any further. Yes, like *right now*. Stop reading, and start writing.)

For some of you, answering this question may feel simple. Your answer might be wanting to finish your daily projects so you can finally go to bed on time for a change. Or maybe you want to squeeze in a run three times a week. Perhaps you want to jack up your productivity so you can get recognized for all the hard work you do and finally get that promotion.

While any of these answers may be factually true, when you look closely at them, they're only surface-deep. If this is how your answers sound, remember that being productive requires a *lasting* change in behavior. Shifting habits takes a ton of effort. Any answer to this vital question that lacks depth, quite simply, will not be enough to motivate you to keep pushing through when the going gets tough.

So, what's the *real* reason you are willing to take on decades of bad habits in an effort to painfully swap them out for new ones? Can you clearly articulate your compelling reason for taking action? Is it powerful enough to keep you motivated when you fall off the productivity wagon, which will inevitably happen as you learn and grow?

Here's my story as an example.

Back in 2003, my wife and I began trying in earnest to have a baby. But it wasn't as easy as taking off the brakes for us. After nine years of praying, hoping, and draining both our bank accounts on IVF attempts, we'd gone through countless miscarriages and a stillborn. We were starting to think it was time to give up on ever being parents.

It was immeasurably difficult on both of us to make this call, but the act of letting go of our decade-long, singular focus had to happen. As it did, it opened us up to the possibility of starting a new chapter in our lives. We decided to refocus our passion for creating something new, and we each began taking steps to launch our respective businesses.

Ironically, four months after choosing this new path, we learned, through some unknown miracle, we were pregnant with a little girl.

After our daughter arrived in this world, I vowed to spend as much time as I could with her. I reworked my schedule so I could work from home full-time. I had worked remotely before with some success, but now

I was *motivated* to make it a productive venture. I didn't decide to become a master of productivity because I needed to save time and make more money because kids ain't cheap (although that's true). No. My reason went deeper. I'd believed fatherhood was off the table for me. Now, that I was given this gift, I was willing to do whatever it took to hoard every second I could, just so I could spend it with my daughter.

Productivity took on a new meaning for me when my daughter was born. My daughter, miracle that she is, *is* my compelling reason.

Every time I want to knock off early, remembering the *real* reason for holding my nose to the grindstone keeps me focused. It helps me remember why I *shouldn't* go down the rabbit hole of chasing emails. It keeps me focused on tasks when I'm just not feeling it that day. It changes the game entirely, every time I think about it.

Your compelling reason will do the same for you.

So, I'll ask again: What is the *real* reason you want to be more productive? Could it be to make more money and put it in your kids' 529 so you can give them the gift of education? Do you want to earn a raise so you can move to a different neighborhood in an effort to change your circumstances? Would you like to have time to volunteer for an organization that resonates with your passion?

Your reason for productivity is yours and yours alone. When you find something you *know* is strong enough to keep you going when things get tough—and trust me, they will—you're ready to move forward.

Once you're clear on your motivation for getting seriously productive, keep reading. In the coming pages, you'll find suggestions to help you reduce and remove your obstacles to productivity, use intervals to hone your focus, and encourage a positive mindset. There's even a section with recommendations just for parents who are working from home.

Some of these productivity tactics are simple. Some are more involved. Try 'em on for size, take the parts you like and use 'em, and leave what doesn't work for you.

20 WAYS TO ROCK YOUR PRODUCTIVITY

PART 1 - Reduce & Remove

1. Reduce Temptation & Remove Barriers: 5:15 Freedom!

5:15 is a simple concept that stands for *5 seconds or less* and *15 seconds or more*. It might just be the ticket to forming or kicking your next habit.

When attempting to form a seemingly daunting habit, such as getting up crazy early every morning to exercise, one of the biggest barriers is often just getting started. Small things get in the way, like finding your shoes and dealing with the whole pesky lace-up situation while you're still half-asleep.

One solution is to make *starting* the task or habit as simple as possible. If you want to exercise every morning, you need to proactively overcome the drag of procrastination you'll inevitably face when choosing a cold floor over your warm bed. So, start by making the activity as easy to initiate as you can.

The night before, place those workout shoes somewhere you can get to them in **5 seconds or less**. Front and center is best: on the toilet lid, in front of the door, in the refrigerator, on top of your alarm clock, wherever. The idea is to put them somewhere that you can't seem to avoid them. In fact, you want it to be almost impossible to ignore them, making it as easy as possible to begin your new habit.

The alternate option, best for when you're trying to break a bad habit (instead of forming a new one), is to put the thing you're trying to avoid in a location that will require you to take at least **15 seconds or more** to get to it. You're trying to make it as annoying or challenging as possible to do or access the thing you are trying to avoid.

Not sure if it'll work? Think about any habit you are trying to break, like looking at your phone too much or eating an entire bag of chips in one sitting. For me, it's not chips—it's brownies. If I put those brownies where I can get to them in five seconds or less, I might easily end up eating half the pan (okay, the whole pan) before I think twice. But if I make it as difficult as possible to get to them (in the very back of the pantry, behind the oatmeal and underneath the unopened pasta, for example), it gives me the time necessary to ask myself, "Should I really be looking this hard for those damn brownies?" I'm *interrupting* my otherwise mindless habit of gorging myself. Besides, out of sight, out of mind, right?

So, bring your good habits closer by giving yourself easy, five-second access, and, to get out of a habit, do the complete opposite. Throw up as many roadblocks and barriers as you possibly can to get "it" at least 15 seconds away from you.

You'll be amazed at how strong your willpower turns out to be.

2. Remove the Unnecessary: The *Eliminator Challenge*

Take a sheet of paper and write down 10 non-essential activities you regularly engage in that require your time, focus, and energy. You are looking for activities that could absolutely be eliminated from your life for an entire week. Be honest with yourself, and think about it like an experiment. Start with obvious activities, like non-work-related social media or random chit-chat with co-workers. Then, dig deeper, and add items that either distract you from your priorities, influence your overall attitude in non-productive ways, or drain your enthusiasm.

Next, for each of the 10 items, also write down a simple solution in parentheses.

For example:

- *Too much Facebook. (Take the app off your phone, and don't log in for seven days.)*

- *Too much TV and video streaming. (Unplug the TV, record shows to watch later, or abstain altogether.)*

- *Chit-chat / idle gossip. (Walk away from these conversations, text threads, or emails.)*

Review your list, and pick three items you could cut out *immediately* for a full seven days. Then, eliminate them, and see what happens.

If you find it hard, cut back to one thing instead of three, and keep trying until you succeed in eliminating that one thing completely for a full week.

If you find it *easy* to eliminate those three things, keep going! Continue ticking things off your list until you've reached your limit or until you've knocked out all 10. Then, make a new list, searching for more things you can eliminate, and repeat the process. Eventually, you'll get to a point where you've eliminated many unnecessary things for two weeks, three weeks, and even longer. At that point, you may find you simply don't need those things in your life at all anymore.

That said, like most habits, it will be uncomfortable at first to make these changes. You may find yourself waffling or reverting back to your favorite modes of distraction. Remember, it's only an experiment, and it's only seven days. If you fall off the wagon a few times, so what? That's to be expected. Just jump back on, and pick up where you left off.

By continually taking the challenge, even if you only eliminate one or two activities per week, you will create space in your daily schedule, and you will reap the benefits of more precious time for yourself.

3. Reduce Your Workload: Employ the EADOR Method

EADOR stands for **E**liminate – **A**utomate – **D**elegate – **O**utsource – **R**efer.

Start by making a bulleted list of every job-related activity you currently perform on a weekly basis—*in detail*. For example: Filling job orders, data research, putting together proposals, attending virtual team meetings, etc. Be sure to also include mundane items, such as responding to emails and phone calls, ordering inventory, posting on social media, scheduling clients, driving to work, processing payroll, etc.

By diving deep into this brain dump, you might be shocked to discover the crazy number of tasks that are eating up your time, day after day, week after week.

Now, using the EADOR process, comb over your task list to determine if any items can be reallocated.

Eliminate: Are there any items no longer worthy of your full attention, time, and effort—enough so that you can eliminate them right off the bat? For example, if you attend six virtual networking functions each month, can you drop at least one of them?

Automate: Usually, there are more than a few items on our weekly task lists that could be automated (for free) to save time, perhaps even a few extra hours every week. Activating auto-response on your email is a prime example. This simple feature can inform people to expect a response from you within 48 hours, thus giving you the freedom to prioritize your replies instead of sitting in front of your computer, feeling trapped as you respond to every email, one by one. If a 48-hour window feels too long, your automated system can direct people to an "emergency only" means of contacting you for a quicker response.

Another great example of automation is using an automated scheduling tool for your calendar, which cuts down on the constant flurry of back-and-forth correspondences when trying to coordinate schedules and meeting times with staff or clients. And, speaking of scheduling, if you use social media for work or to promote a business, you can schedule out your posts days, weeks, and even months in advance, either within the platform you're using or with a third-party scheduling tool.

Delegate: It can be challenging to let go of important tasks you've always handled yourself, even if you've got a reliable, helpful team. But delegating to others is an obvious way to reduce your workload and work more effectively. *(If you don't have any staff to whom you can delegate, keep reading—there's more for you farther down this list of tactics.)*

Identify those tasks that do not require your expertise or talent, such as setting up appointments, responding to non-critical emails, or culling through research data, and explore the possibility of passing such activities along to capable team members who are willing and available to help you.

Outsource: Thanks to online platforms like Upwork, you can cost-effectively search for a freelancer to whom you can outsource certain tasks or projects (presuming it's acceptable to do so within your company/team). When considering this option, identify tasks you don't need to do, don't want to do, or that would be better suited for someone more/differently qualified, and seek out a resource to help. Online platforms make it easy to find transcribers, videographers, graphic artists, and much, much more. They can also handle your project flow and serve as a means of securing dialogue with contractors. You can ask for RFP's (Requests For Proposals) from multiple vendors, and then select the ones best-suited for your particular needs.

Likewise, VAs (virtual assistants) can be a godsend when it comes to taking on dreaded tasks like scheduling meetings and making travel arrangements. Some VAs even have advanced credentials and are capable of handling more complex tasks such as project management, billing, and bookkeeping. (These highly prized individuals can be found by utilizing some of the search functions on LinkedIn.)

Refer: This activity is specifically relevant if you interact directly with clients. If your schedule is maxed out, or if you happen to encounter someone who is simply not a good fit for your business or style, consider referring them to trusted colleagues both inside and outside your company. As long as you use good judgment when entering into these arrangements and are intentional and careful with your referrals, these strategic relationships can, over time, grow into fruitful, reciprocal referral partnerships.

To conclude the EADOR method, identify which action on your EADOR list is the easiest to complete, and start with that one item. Be sure to allocate an appropriate amount of time, and mark it in your calendar. Then, get to work breaking free of the "I have to do it all myself" mindset. Remember, letting go is one of the fastest ways to getting more of your time!

4. Reduce, Tally, and Get a Room

There's no question remote working comes with plenty of distractions to ruin your focus. So, let's get rid of them… or at least some of them.

Start by taking out a piece of paper and writing down your three biggest distractions, the things that often interrupt the flow of your workday. Some distractions on your list will be created by other people: the doorbell ringing, your kids playing (or arguing) loudly, incoming calls and emails. Some distractions will be things you create yourself (oops): surfing YouTube, checking the fridge, or texting a friend.

Once you've written down your top three distractions, including at least one self-created distraction, get a sticky note and put it beside your laptop. Divide your sticky into thirds lengthwise to create three columns. Assign each of your three main distractions a column by writing it at the top. Throughout your day, every time you get distracted by one of the items on your sticky note, put a tick mark in the respective column. At the end of the day, tally how many times you were distracted by each respective thing.

Now, choose one of the three distractions, maybe the one that interrupted you most. Come up with several creative solutions that will reduce the frequency and duration of that particular distraction. Implement your solution(s) immediately, and track your results the following day.

Keep repeating this exercise with each thing on your list, and see how many distractions you can reduce.

As a final resort, if you truly need a moment of peace, *now*, and you don't have the time or bandwidth to tally and experiment, you can always try physically removing yourself from the chaos by "getting a room."

When you work from home or in close proximity to others, it can be nearly impossible to create a quiet, distraction-free work space unless you get creative. At home, try grabbing an unoccupied bedroom, or, if you're really desperate, a closet. There have even been times when my only choice was to use my car, which I did, gladly. Or maybe you have the option of going to your deserted office building occasionally, allowing you to literally get away for a while. Bottom line, if you force yourself to create a fortress of solitude, you can sequester yourself there to focus on work (at least until someone finds you).

5. Reduce Priorities: The One Thing

I like to pick a time, usually first thing in the morning, and write down three to five things I would like to accomplish during my workday. I make sure these things have a *direct* impact on my success in the *future*, i.e. will further my job, my career, or move my business in the direction of growth. For example, in my line of work, my "future success today" list might include making six follow-up calls with prospective clients, finishing the web page promoting our upcoming webinar, or preparing for a strategic partner call. For others in a different field, the list might be tasks related to staff training, taking a course for a credential, or test-driving project management software platforms. Whatever they are for you, make sure these three to five tasks have a direct impact on your *future* success.

After I have written my list, I circle the single, most important task to accomplish that day. This is **the one thing** that will have the greatest impact on my future success. Even if my day blows up, I make sure that specific task is knocked out. That way, I still know I'm moving in the right direction.

6. Reduce Stimulation: Turn Off the *Dumbphone*

The biggest distraction for most people nowadays is the smartphone, or as I often call it, the dumbphone. It's impossible to focus on *anything* if you are continuously interrupted by an electronic device ringing, jingling, tingling, and vibrating, tempting you to check texts and emails, which inevitably also means replying to texts and emails, which leads to nine million other distractions. Once you're sucked in, breaking free is a massive battle.

However, the solution is right there in the palm of your hand: the *off button*. Press down… Hold for three full seconds… There you go. Keep your phone off for at least 45 minutes, or however long you need to complete the task at hand.

PART 2 - Hone Your Focus

7. Create Keystone Habits

Not all habits are created equal. Some have far more impact than others. If you're going to put in the notable effort required to break bad habits and create new, productive ones, you're going to want the most bang for your buck, right? Here's how to make that happen. Pull out your pen and paper, and answer this question (yes, right now):

> *What is one habit that, once mastered, would be a total game changer for you?*

Typically, I hear responses like, "Talking to one new potential client every day," or "Knocking out my single most important project every day, before I do anything else." While these kinds of behavioral habits will definitely help drive you to greater success, they often aren't enough to provoke deep change in your life. To achieve lasting change (the kind many of us are looking for!), you want to establish a *keystone habit.*

Simply put, a keystone habit is a beneficial activity performed on a regular basis (i.e. habitually) *that gives rise to other beneficial habits.* When executed with dogmatic vigor, a keystone habit can powerfully change the course of your life.

I'll illustrate this phenomenon by sharing the experience of a client of mine, Kelly.

For some time, Kelly had been talking about establishing an exercise regimen for herself, ideally working out three times a week. She had attempted to incorporate this routine into her weekly schedule, but she found it impossible to keep up with it on a regular basis. Kelly is a highly disciplined individual overall, and rarely, if ever, leaves items on her to-do list undone.

So her lack of follow-through on this particular goal was a thorn in her side. She was primed to add this new item to her list, but her work schedule was so overloaded, she simply couldn't find time to add in three exercise sessions each week.

A notable detail: As much as Kelly knew she needed to exercise, it wasn't something she *enjoyed* doing. She knew it would result in her shedding a few pounds, and that she'd feel better overall, but she hadn't considered the possible benefits of a habitual exercise regimen beyond the direct benefits of exercise itself.

I asked Kelly, "How might this exercise habit create opportunities for the formation of *other* useful habits in your life?"

Within just a few moments, she came up with a plethora of enthusiastic answers. "If I'm exercising regularly, I'll be more inclined to improve my eating habits overall," she mused. "I can download some business books I've been meaning to read, and I can listen to them while I'm working out. Committing to an exercise regimen will require revamping my schedule, which will ultimately improve my time management skills. Oh! And I'll start my day in a great mood, which will improve my whole outlook for the entire day."

"By establishing the habit of doing something I *need* to do for myself, even if I don't particularly *want* to do it, I'll be creating a template for tackling tasks I don't like to do at work, too. I'll probably get *more* done than before, with less work and in less time!"

Kelly's enthusiasm and list of benefits just kept on growing from there, giving her ample reason to reprioritize her exercise regimen. Now, instead of remaining on the hamster wheel, stuck in a pattern of putting the needs of others before her own, it was abundantly clear she had to put herself first. By creating a habit of exercising on a regular basis for *herself*, she could easily unlock an entirely new lifestyle.

In the end, this particular keystone habit (regularly exercising) ended up being the *perfect* habit for Kelly and her situation. Adding it to her plate forced her to finally create some much needed "me time," which helped reset and improve just about every other part of her life.

Do you need a little "me time" right now, just like Kelly did? Keystone habits often involve taking action to meet your personal needs in order to free you to embrace other positive habits and choices, too. Just remember that exercise is only one example. Maybe you've been wanting to read more, meditate every day, or walk the dog more frequently. Whatever you choose, making time for *you* isn't unproductive. In fact, when you are working your butt off in a cramped space while trying to care for other human beings and also dealing with all the other wonky things going on in our world, it might be the most productive choice of all.

8. Use a Tomato to Help You Focus (yes, seriously)

The Italian word *pomodoro* means *tomato*, and the Pomodoro Technique is a simple yet brilliant strategy to increase one's focus. The technique was created in the late 1980's by an Italian university student who needed to get his distractibility under control and increase his ability to focus over extended periods of time. So, using a novelty kitchen timer shaped like a tomato, he came up with a simple system for consistently achieving more focus and productivity. His approach is especially useful when tackling a lengthy project, such as writing a book or working out logistics for a new product launch.

Here are the basics of the Pomodoro Method:

1. **Select a task.**

    Break your biggest project down into a series of small tasks. Let's say you've been asked to help find more staff to run a new regional territory your company acquired. Your initial task list might include:

    - Pulling together all the resources necessary for recruiting

    - Compiling, creating, and organizing the paperwork and procedures for new-hire onboarding

- Coordinating the necessary training curriculum for these new positions

Decide which of these smaller tasks you'd like to tackle first.

2. **Work for 25 minutes.**

   Set a timer for 25 minutes. (The original *Pomodoro Technique* suggests using a ticking timer to add a sense of urgency.) During the 25 minutes, you are to focus *solely* on your task at hand. No distractions!

3. **Take a break.**

   When the timer goes off, stop working. If you're in mid-thought, make a note of the essential point with only a few words, just enough so you won't forget it, and then take a break for five minutes to give your mind a rest.

4. **Repeat the cycle.**

   Set the timer for another 25 minutes, and repeat Step 2.

5. **Continue in "sets."**

   Implement this "work + break" cycle up to four times. After the fourth cycle, take a break for a full 20 minutes, representing the end of one set. Continue until you've completed the task.

To get the most out of this technique, select a distraction-free environment to conduct your *Pomodori* (as multiple work + break cycles are called), such as a vacant room, a quiet (closed-door) home office, or even your parked car. If you get distracted in the middle of one of your *Pomodori,* even for a moment, stop, take a short break, and start the cycle again.

To learn more about the *Pomodoro Technique* and why it works, read more: www.pomodorotechnique.com.

9. Forget the Tomato: Make Your Own Intervals

Remember, I am an ADHD poster child. So when anyone asks me if I can focus for hours on end, I laugh out loud and respond, "I'm more of a sprinter than a marathoner." Focusing for short bursts of time works best for me.

Knowing focus is a challenge, I've spent a lot of time and effort working on it. These days, I can go for about 50 minutes, and then I *must* take a 10-minute break. If I do two or three cycles of focus time, break time, focus time, break time, I've learned I can stay on task for most of the day.

If that sounds dauntingly long to you, don't worry. My ability to remain focused and productive for such stretches of time didn't happen overnight; I had to build up to it. When I first started working with the "interval technique," I could only last 10, maybe 15 minutes before my mind started wandering. The 25-minute intervals recommended in the popular Pomodoro Technique (#7, above) were too long; I felt defeated when I consistently fell short of my focus goal.

So, I decided to forget the tomato and create my own intervals. I started small, with short, 10-minute bursts. Over time, I practiced, gradually increasing the length of my focus blocks. Today, 45 to 50 minutes is my norm (so I'm still not using the Pomodoro approach!).

If the Pomodoro way isn't right for you, that's okay. You may just need a shorter (or longer) interval. Experiment with different combinations of focus/break intervals, and see what works best for you.

10. Checking Email: Timing Is Everything

Email sucks the life out of me. By the time I've answered one email, five more have landed in the inbox; within a few minutes, my ability to focus has completely waned, and my thoughts are shooting in a multitude of directions.

The most successful technique I've discovered for staying on track is to *refrain from checking email at the beginning of my workday* and to instead spend that time generating my to-do list and organizing my itinerary for the day.

When I finally dive into email, I tackle my *outgoing* list first, not my inbox. I send out emails following up with prospective and current clients because, based on those eventual responses, I'll have more information for planning (and possibly altering) my day.

For the rest of the day, I also check my email only at specific times. I've designated four times throughout my day to pop into my inbox and clear it out. Doing this forces me to get through my emails faster and move on to the next task on my list.

If you've grown accustomed to checking email all day long, four times a day might feel impossible at first. Try weaning yourself down first, checking email every hour on the hour, and gradually lengthen the time in between.

11. Research Says: Take a Break

If you are driven by an over-the-top work ethic and are always on the lookout for gaining a competitive edge, consider indulging in something your competition probably hasn't considered: taking more breaks.

In the book, "*Peak Performance: Elevate Your Game, Avoid Burnout, and Thrive with the New Science of Success,*" by Brad Stulberg and Steve Magness, they discuss a simple formula: *stress + rest = growth*. Simply stated, in order to achieve optimal growth in any endeavor, a stress period must occur, which is then followed by a rest period.

In weightlifting, for example, if the resistance isn't heavy enough, the muscles will not be worked enough to grow. To achieve optimal muscle growth, the stress load must be high enough to effectively challenge the muscles. At the same time, though, the muscles cannot be overloaded beyond capacity. Too much stress load, and the result is muscle failure or injury.

While you may not be a weightlifter working your physical muscles, there is no question you are under stress. All those projects, tasks, and deliverables on your plate are currently stressing *you*. That's not necessarily a bad thing—as long as you, like fitness enthusiasts everywhere, periodically step back from the stress to rest, too. Too much stress leads to burnout. Too little stress, or too much rest, can lead to stagnation. The solution is striking a balance between the two.

Fortunately for all my fellow Type-A's out there who refuse to take a break without seeing hard evidence proving it's necessary, there's data proving adequate breaks are not only refreshing for the brain, they're actually *enhancing*.

In a study that analyzed the effects of taking regularly scheduled breaks, people who customarily worked 70 to 80 hours a week for a competitive consulting company were asked to take regular breaks. These orders to take breaks were given *even though these teammates had stated they were convinced that if they didn't consistently work as hard as possible for as long as possible, it would result in the loss of millions of dollars for the business*—which would lead to their termination.

In this high stakes experiment, staffers were required to turn off their email after 8PM and commit to not working at least one night per week. Many employees and their respective managers worried that performance levels and production volume would drop.

However, after a month of implementing this practice, the quality of ideas and production volume had improved appreciably, resulting in a net *gain* of contracts—*not* a loss.

When people applied rest, they effectively re-invigorated their drained brains. Because of it, they were able to perform at higher cognitive levels, without mental burnout.

So how much rest is the right amount? As a general rule, the greater the stress you're under, the more rest you'll need. If you work on a major project that requires multiple weeks of undivided attention, it makes sense, once the project is completed, to schedule an extended holiday, or at least a weekend getaway, to allow full recovery for your battered brain and body. For smaller projects, such as writing an article or putting together a sales proposal, using an interval approach (where you work for a specific period of time, then take a short break before resuming work) might be enough.

Remember, most of us are *not* suffering from not working long enough or hard enough. The inverse is true. You can still work hard, but be sure to take a break. Intentional rest periods will increase your productivity in both the short and long term.

PART 3 - Be Present

12. Double Down During DO NOT DISTURB Time

Prioritizing your to-do list gives you the best shot at maximizing productivity. But there are often unexpected variables to deal with, like a frantic phone call from a client whose deadline just got pushed up and who needs the proposal from you by the end of today, not tomorrow, as originally planned.

When I need to seriously focus, I reach out to friends, colleagues, and family members. I let them know I need a bracketed period of uninterrupted time that will allow me to tackle that non-negotiable project, the one that has to get done *now*. Knowing I only have a specific amount of time before the distractions come raining back in forces me to focus, and I can often knock out a project in just one or two hours.

Remember, if you need to send a Do Not Disturb message or request to your boss or co-workers, be extra-mindful of their position in the company and their schedules as you clarify your boundaries.

Expert tip: This productivity tactic works best when you plan ahead. Mapping out an appropriate, workable system (think DND sign on your home office door like they do at the hotels) for designated Do Not Disturb times is best done during calm moments, not the middle of your time crunch crisis. Emergencies happen, and knowing how you'll respond will help keep you on track when they do.

13. Quitting Time: Hard Stop & Unplug

My mind is easily distracted by the bombardment of emails, texts, documents to read, and the cacophony of sound spewing from television sets and radios everywhere I go. Furthermore, my job necessitates juggling a wide spectrum of personalities and emotional states on a daily basis. I frequently deal with upset clients, demanding family members, and even needy pets (for cryin' out loud!).

Before I knew what I know now, I attempted to remedy my agitation by spending countless hours on the sofa, drooling in front of the TV, clutching all kinds of adult beverages, and soaking in mindless programs. I imagined this regimen would somehow help me relax and recharge. Really, though, it only made things worse. Night after night, I found myself lying in bed, staring at the ceiling with my mind racing, unable to get a full night's sleep, and waking up the next morning with a headache and a bad attitude.

What I needed was a way to give my "work brain" a rest so I could wake up in the morning refreshed and ready to take on the world.

The solution was simple, although it eluded me for many of my work-from-home years: I needed a designated quitting time each day, followed by a big slice of "unplugged time." So, that's exactly what I did. Having watched my bad habits for years, my wife was totally on board, and it didn't hurt that she reaped the benefits as much as I did. Imagine having dinner with your family without phones, TV or music. It leaves you no choice but to actually talk and connect with the people you care most about, which is something many of us complain we never have time for. In fact, ever since our family consciously designated dinner time as "unplugged time," our relationships have grown notably deeper.

Having a designated quitting time also solved the problem of getting my mind to calm down when it's time for sleep. Now, about 30 minutes before we turn in for the night, I enjoy quiet conversations with my wife about our family, about the good things that happened to us that day, really about anything—as long as it's positive and not about work. Doing so puts a smile on both our faces and lands us in a very grateful state of mind, perfectly conducive to a full night's rest.

These days I find, almost without exception, that I wake up recharged and re-focused, with a wonderfully positive attitude about the day and my life. Try unplugging, and see what it can do for you.

14. Soak It In: Enjoy the Moment

Many people lead hectic lives, and I am definitely one of those people. Regardless of your lifestyle, it can be hard to find a few moments of peace and quiet during the day. However, there's probably an oasis you can find somewhere between wake-up time and bedtime.

For me, my moment of quiet happens early in the morning. For a few minutes every day, while my family is still asleep, I take time for myself to just sit on the deck with a cup of coffee. During these brief moments, I clear my head by breathing deeply, soaking in the morning sun, noticing the trees and the different types of songbirds I can hear. Not only does this simple ritual help me appreciate the moment, it also serves to ground and center me before I dive into my day.

I've also learned to use this same technique to calm my nerves and get my head in the game before a big presentation or an important client meeting. You can even combine this technique with the Pomodoro Method (#7, above), enjoying a moment of presence during one of your interval break times.

15. Shhh: Shut Up and Listen

This 10-minute activity is a great way to train yourself to be a more present listener, and it can have a huge impact on how you interact with clients and colleagues. You'll need a partner for this one, and it's advisable to practice with a good friend or significant other before experimenting with clients.

To start, you'll want to carve out a *relaxed* 10-minute window when you're not scheduled to be anywhere for at least half an hour. Having a relaxed state of mind is key. Prepare yourself to open up a topic of conversation your partner cares deeply about. You can ask them about a special project they've been planning, a field of study they're passionate about, or even an interpersonal conflict they've been trying to work out. The important thing is that *they* genuinely care about the topic and *you* are 100% focused on them, with no distractions whatsoever. Your goal is *pure listening*.

Over time, this exercise will vastly improve your ability to be present and connected, deepening the relationships with people you care about, including family, friends, and clients.

Expert tip: Practicing this technique regularly has the added benefit of making the WILSSN method (Chapter 3) even more effective.

16. Positive Mindset: Feed Your Head Good "Food"

We all know what happens if we feed our bodies a steady stream of junk food. Conversely, we are also aware of the benefits of healthy food options. But we don't often think about how we're feeding our minds.

What would happen if you started changing the way you "feed your head?" What if you were to steer clear of pettiness and negativity in your daily interactions? If you did your best to only engage in positive, productive conversations? What would happen if you consumed a steady regimen of motivational articles and productive videos instead of binging on mind-dulling television programs or doom-scrolling down your news feed?

Becoming aware of what you're putting into your head doesn't mean you have to disconnect from the world completely. But being willing to revamp your "diet" for the better can have a profound, positive effect on your attitude, your outlook on life, and your productivity. Give it a try, and see what happens for you.

PART 4 - Just for Parents

Parents,

If you are new to working remotely, and you suddenly have kids running around your "office" every day, it's likely you are questioning your sanity. Even pre-pandemic, for many, working from home meant struggling to get anything done. Now, we've added the challenges of daytime nannying and homeschooling while dealing with a constantly changing world.

Of course, fixing the world's problems is going to take more than a few productivity hacks. But the next four productivity strategies, meant specifically for parents, will *help you manage the kiddo craziness at home, stay productive "at work," and keep yourself from going insane.*

17. Get on the Same Page: Try a Morning "Parent Huddle"

When the lock-down happened, and kids were sent home, for the first two weeks, my wife Amanda and I kept our old routine. We'd wake up early, make our to-do lists, and get a good workout in before tackling our day, just as we'd done for years. However, we were now facing a problem: When our seven-year-old daughter came crashing downstairs each morning and saw both Mommy and Daddy at home, she assumed it was the weekend, meaning it was time to play, not to study and learn.

The biggest problem was how to integrate remote learning into the rest of our day-to-day craziness. Which subject would be taught by whom? What about the work calls we both had scheduled? What food did we have in the fridge, and who would be responsible for making lunch? The idea of remote learning was brand new to us, and, since neither Amanda nor I have any experience with home-schooling, we were forced to make it up as we went along. It wasn't long before voices were raised and feelings were hurt.

Our failure to communicate needs and expectations caused plenty of arguments. Finally, we figured out that we each had an idea about how our workday was supposed to flow, but we had never shared that with each other because, before lock-down, it had never been necessary to do so.

So, here's our new daily program: After we're done with our morning routines, we come together for a *Parent Huddle*: a 30-minute meeting where we go over our respective work schedules, the household schedule, and our priorities for the day. We discuss our timing for homeschooling our daughter, for our virtual meetings, and for housework. Together, we decide who will be doing what, and when.

Lastly, and just as importantly, we communicate to our daughter just how important this morning meeting is. By keeping our daughter in the loop—telling her that we're in a meeting, that we need some privacy, and that we'll be done by 8:30 AM—helps her relax into the day, too. (Remember, this is a whole new program for our kids, too, and they're just as discombobulated as the rest of us!)

Miraculously, establishing this morning huddle completely snapped our daughter out of the notion that this new daytime arrangement meant we were living in a perpetual weekend. Because we do have this meeting every weekday morning, it sets the tone that "today is a *workday*," and she happily complies (most of the time).

18. Off Limits: Get Out of My Office!

New to this whole "WFH" (Working From Home) concept, for Amanda, the first few weeks of quarantine were more WTF than WFH. Her main source of frustration came from the interruptions from our daughter that inevitably ensued within 20 minutes of Amanda opening her laptop. Whether tasked with tracking down a roll of Scotch tape for a crafting project or asked (more than a few times) to demonstrate the pronunciation of a tricky word from a study book, there's always *something* pulling Amanda's attention away from work. In a very short time, this naturally left her feeling frustrated and unproductive.

Fortunately for me, over the years, I've implemented a firm *Daddy WFH Protocol* for my daughter. She knows I mean business when I tell her, "Unless it's an emergency, please don't disturb me when I'm in my office." Usually, she has no trouble. However, it was a different story for Amanda. Seeing Mom at home during the day has always cued *playtime*. Thus, when suddenly Mom was home all the time, our daughter had trouble grasping the concept of not interrupting.

Since "Dad's office" is synonymous with "do not disturb," we moved Amanda into my office during work hours. Within a week, our daughter adapted and understood that even though Mom is home, it's not playtime. If she's in Dad's office, Mom is *working*.

Even better, now that she knows Mom is not available while she's working, Amanda is free to move her workspace elsewhere in the house rather than be held hostage in my office in order to work without interruption.

19. Straight Talk: Ditch the Guilt

For years, when Amanda left the house for work every day, she felt like a bad parent. It was the classic heartache scenario of Mom driving off, watching her daughter in the rearview mirror, waving goodbye with tears streaming down her precious little face.

When a mandatory quarantine was ordered and Amanda was forced to work from home, that painful memory surged forward every time our daughter asked for her attention—even if it was only for a brief moment. I watched Amanda as she became seriously torn between doing her client work and spending time with her kid, and I felt guilty for not noticing this dilemma earlier.

So Amanda and I sat down and had some straight talk about a few hard realities we hadn't yet fully acknowledged, much less embraced. (In all fairness, our heads were spinning, just trying to get a handle on what was actually going on in the world, and in our world. Of course, in many ways, we continue to navigate this.)

Tough truths we finally put our finger on:

1. Amanda was now a Work-From-Home parent. That was a HUGE adjustment to make in her thinking and frankly more than just a little bit of a shock.

2. The whole *daughter-is-here-but-I-must-work* guilt was not something Amanda had previously ever had to consider or navigate, and it was uncomfortable for her to get her head around.

3. For years now, our little one has functioned *very well* during the week without hours of Amanda's undivided attention. She has absolutely demonstrated the ability to entertain herself for 60-minute stretches while I'm working. Understanding this was pivotal in helping Amanda to let go of the guilt.

Our reality check chat helped in many ways, and now Amanda finds it much easier to stick to her work-related tasks, even when our daughter vies for her attention. She has cultivated her ability to say, "It's not a good time right now," without feeling guilty. She's also learned to ask for my help in redirecting our child when she needs to put in a few solid work hours with-out distraction (#12, above).

Most importantly, identifying these truths and discussing them helped us all find greater acceptance of our lives and circumstances as they are now.

20. Stay Flexible: Live, Don't Die, by a Schedule

Without a schedule, you're adding the element of uncertainty to your days, weeks and months. As we all know having gone through a pandemic, the more uncertainty we feel, the more anxious about the future we become. Fortunately, predictability is a beautiful gift that you can give yourself and your family at any time by creating a regular family schedule.

Our daughter has always thrived in the structured environment provided by her school, but when that was put on hold, she soon became prone to stubbornness and starting arguments. She also became far less interested in activities she previously loved. Noticing this, Amanda and I, who guard our schedules like bulldogs and have spent years practicing healthy personal and professional time boundaries, decided we needed to create a schedule to accommodate *all* of our family's needs.

The new family schedule hinges on the concept of *on-duty* and *off-duty*. At any time, the off-duty parent is free to conduct business during designated blocks of times, doled out in half-day or whole-day increments. When that parent is working, the on-duty parent is knocking out household chores and engaging with our daughter, whose day is structured around blocks of time dedicated to class time, play time (on FaceTime), and free time (for drawing, riding her bike, or playing outside).

By officially structuring and alternating our on-and-off duty blocks throughout the week, Amanda and I have a better handle on our work, and our family has settled into a steady rhythm.

All that said, we know and accept that this strategy is far from perfect. There are way too many unpredictable elements in our world to strive for perfection. Although we're slowly getting the hang of this home-schooling thing, our daughter's teachers often surprise us with supplementary live video lessons at odd times for the purpose of keeping students engaged. Amanda and I have also noticed our clients scrambling to accommodate *their* shifting workloads and *their* new family obligations, and our schedules do not always line up as planned. The truth is, *everyone* is affected by what has changed, and *everyone* finds it challenging to stick to a hard-and-fast schedule these days.

But that doesn't mean you should just give up. Here are a few tweaks Amanda and I made to our scheduling practices as we learned what worked and what didn't.

Sharing our online work calendars with each other was helpful. It allowed us to coordinate a few predictable slots on our respective calendars. However, scheduling a longer time slot of four hours or more, with the intention of knocking out our larger tasks, was impossible. We realized right away it was *never* going to happen, so now we don't even try. Instead, we look for *pockets of time* to accomplish small portions of larger tasks and projects. For example, if I know our daughter is doing her online Spanish class for 30 minutes, I use that time to bang out a few paragraphs of an article. Or if I'm on daughter duty, and Amanda gets an unexpected opening in her schedule due to a client canceling, I'll ask her for a tag-out so I can grab a few more minutes and nail a few more paragraphs.

Sure, it's less than ideal, but it's working for us, as long as we continue to communicate with each other.

* * *

In the end, we all need to remember that juggling work tasks, providing home-schooling, and maintaining a harmonious household in close confinement, all while trying to stay upbeat during a dark chapter in your personal life and/or human history, is not easy! I still struggle to comprehend how much my world, Amanda's world, our daughter's world, and I'm sure *your* world, has changed, and so quickly.

I'll leave you with this thought. Last week, after a particularly rough day, I was putting our daughter to bed. As I tucked her in, I asked her a simple question. "What is one thing I could do that would help me be a better Daddy?" I asked.

In a quiet voice, she replied, "Just be patient with me."

Sage advice for us all.

BUNNY

I won't even pretend productivity hacks are my jam; you already know Chris has all the productivity techniques you could ask for. But I will offer some perspective and psychology, which underpins all those practical methods and approaches you've just read.

Since Chris started with a definition, I'll do the same, even though our definitions don't exactly match (no surprise). Dictionary aside, I define productivity as "not doing unnecessary things." Which, it turns out, means many, many things. If you can agree with me on that, we're doing great so far.

Now, look at your calendar for the next week. Go ahead, open it. This book will wait while you do.

What do you see? Do you see any "unnecessary" things on there? Things that maybe don't really add value to your life?

Next, scroll four to six weeks out. Do you see some open time? Places where you haven't scheduled anything yet? Those empty spots are my favorite times on everyone's calendar. They are what I like to call "change space" because they are where change has the potential to happen.

It's up to you if it will, though. Do you want to make a change? Or are you totally content with your life, your work, and where you are right now?

Most of us are not totally happy with our lives. There are things we want to improve, things we talk about changing. But the thing is, we rarely *actually* change.

Instead, we complain that we're "too busy" to make changes, big or small. Caught up in everything happening in our lives, we tell ourselves we don't have time to take advantage of opportunities. We feel like we don't even have the brain space to *consider* making a change, much less seeing one through.

But the reality is that we are not too busy. We are overbooked with commitments that should never have made their way onto our calendars. Our time is filled up by all kinds of nonsense that aren't actually priorities at all. They are just things we committed to doing, yes after yes after yes that should have been a no.

Maybe I'm wrong. Maybe everything you do really is necessary, a true reflection of your priorities. But if you're like the majority of humans, and that's not the case… If you keep living your life in "too busy" mode… If you keep going like you are going, with no rest and no end in sight… It *will* lead to burnout. I guarantee it.

Now is the time to stop doing unproductive, unnecessary things.

Remote or not, the biggest problem I see with our productivity is that we are repeating the same time-consuming activities over and over. And far too often, they are unnecessary. They are not value-adding activities or things that make a real difference. They are not the best use of our precious time. And the biggest bummer of all is all these auto-piloted activities end up stealing time away from our families and ourselves. Our true priorities somehow always end up on the back burner or at the bottom of the list.

Fortunately, as we identified on your calendar just a few moments ago, there *is* space for change. You may have to look a few weeks out, but time and space are available, and anything is possible when you intentionally devote the time and energy. Remember, success is not about the stars lining up or getting lucky. Anyone who is successful will tell you it took hard work and time, invested repeatedly, despite the highs and lows along the way for them to get there.

So, rather than wait until the action section (because, thanks to Chris' list of productivity hacks, your homework is pretty obvious) let's go back to your calendar right now. Look again at that week where you saw available "change space." Right now, before *anything* else creeps in and steals that time, I want you to go ahead and schedule one of each of the following:

- An hour for self-care (yoga, a walk, meditating, reading, gardening, or whatever lights you up inside).

- An hour of time blocked off for one (just one!) "can we meet for coffee (via Zoom)?" meeting.

- Two nights where you will come home, leave the laptop at the office or in the car, and hide your phone in a basket or drawer until morning.

- One half-day off work, and I mean *OFF*. Do family stuff, combine it with your self-care, visit a place you have never been, whatever. Just block it off, right now.

- An hour of continuing education. Read those articles you keep marking unread in your email box, look up a publication from your favorite professional association, or educate yourself with anything from Tim Ferriss.

If you put these five things in your calendar right now, you will be on your way to a more successful week than any other week in your calendar.

Why? By putting calendar blocks in place, you are far more likely to actually do these activities than when you just tell yourself, "I'll practice some self-care during that time—unless a client wants something, or I don't finish that project in time, or my son needs me. Then I'll just push it back until next week."

Looking far enough out to find "change space" on your calendar and making the choice right now as to how you will use it also guarantees you some down time to rest and recharge, which, if you've read Chris' section above, you now know is pretty damn important. Plus, enjoying some free time could lead you on a new adventure that will give you valuable perspective. Because of your self-care, when you get started on work again, you will have new energy. You'll also have improved clarity, which, as I know from both personal and professional experience, always leads to greater results.

Still unsure about filling your calendar up with these types of change activities? Not a problem. You do not have to do this every week. I am only asking you to try this for one week, like an experiment. If it does not work, and you do not notice a difference, tweak your approach. Find five different things you can put on your calendar, and try again.

If you're not sure what you want to try, here's a pro tip. In an interview with "Side Hustle Guru" Susie Moore, she suggested, when presented with a choice for putting something on your calendar, to always make the choice that feels like freedom, that you are drawn to, and about which you're most passionate.

With change on your calendar, you can actually get started living your best life.

TAKE ACTION!

Just Do It *(Chris)*

You have 20 ways to get more productive, plus a bonus lesson on how to hack your calendar for more self-care. If these tactics sound like they just might change your life, don't get so excited that you try them all at one. Pace yourself!

Pick two productivity hacks and implement them over the next week. The following week, pick another two to implement, and so on. Mix and match and tweak them a little to fit your unique situation.

Remember: Changing routines and behavioral habits is hard! Keep coming back to the real reason you want to be more productive, and get back on that horse. You will get there eventually.

Journal It Out *(Bunny)*

What is one thought or concept you took away from this chapter?

Did any familiar themes, fears, or habits of thought come up for you as you read this chapter? Do any of these patterns have the power to limit your progress? If so, how could you alter your thinking and reframe those thoughts to keep you moving forward?

Right now I am feeling:
_____

The first two productivity hacks I will implement this week are _____ and _____.

Midway check-in: On a scale from 1-10, how confident are you in your ability to be productive while working remotely?

CHAPTER 6:
THINK 🧠 LIKE A BOSS

CHRIS

Remote work is booming. It's so popular it has caused a real estate trend known as "Zoom towns," named for the abundance of people who have moved to picturesque locations thanks to their new ability to telework via Zoom, the video conferencing platform. One such place is a beautiful mountain town called Truckee, California. Nestled in between the trees and rocks on the northern side of famous Lake Tahoe, it's an outdoors lovers' mecca, ideal for those who enjoy snow sports, hiking, mountain biking, sailing, paddle boarding… you name it.

Fleeing from large cities like San Francisco in an attempt to escape the plague and embracing the remote working lifestyle, these newcomers began arriving in droves when the pandemic hit. In fact, according to real estate brokerage website Redfin, the housing market in Truckee alone jumped a whopping 23% from 2019 to 2020.

The advantages of the Zoomtown lifestyle are obvious: stunning scenery, abundant time with your family, and easy access to your hobbies and passions. However, as we've already discussed, remote work also comes with its disadvantages. We've addressed work-from-home productivity challenges, but what about the fact that you no longer have a boss around the office? A good boss helps you prioritize projects, stay on task, and take advantage of resources at your disposal. They provide deadlines and feedback on your overall performance. A great boss also guides you to be more thoughtful when approaching challenging colleagues and clients. They help you learn from your mistakes and understand the virtues of being 100% accountable for your results. Ultimately, your boss gives you the necessary tools to make better decisions (more on that in a sec).

But now, there is no boss in the office next door.

Of course, you can probably still reach your boss via call or Zoom, but if you're used to having someone *right there* and are struggling without that close support, there's good news. You still have access to the best boss ever, *the boss that lives in the six inches between your ears*. Now that you've been kinda-sorta promoted to being at-home executive, let's dive into the biggest challenge you might not even realize exists in your remote work world.

When it comes to making decisions, without even realizing it, most of us implement a flawed and habitual process called *confirmation bias*. Instead of treating each new situation as unique, we allow our past experiences to influence our final choice… even if it's not the best option available.

Confirmation bias happens when we make a certain decision in the present because we're convinced we already know what will happen. We believe we have the answer because of what occurred in a similar situation in the past… even if it wasn't a hundred percent relevant to the current situation. Wielding a surprising amount of influence over us, confirmation bias can lead us to dismiss the opinions and perspectives of others and even reject sound points we'd do well to consider.

One way to avoid confirmation bias is to shift your mindset, and to do so, there's one approach in particular I love because it's wildly effective, and that's the scientific method. Maybe you remember the scientific method at a high level from science class: You come up with a hypothesis, gather evidence to support your hunch, and then run a variety of experiments until you get the results you want. If you're able to repeat your results a few times over, you have "proven" your hypothesis.

While this version of the method is seamlessly integrated into our every day reasoning, it is actually an incomplete understanding of how the scientific method is intended to work. Ironically, as scientifically sound as it appears, this half-correct approach often leads directly to confirmation basis.

For the scientific method to truly work as intended, providing objective truths and verifiable outcomes, we must employ the *entire* scientific method. We must be sure to include a particularly critical part of the process that most of us tend to skip over in daily life: When dealing with a hypothesis, gathering evidence, and collecting data, the scientific method *requires* that we intentionally seek out information that might disprove the desired outcome, not just data that supports our assumptions. Essentially, we have to approach the investigation from the other side, going to extreme lengths to prove ourselves wrong. Only with this level of scrutiny will there be any validity or correctness to your conclusions.

Here is a personal example of this method in action. A while back, I was involved in a project featuring online payment processing. Our platform design team became embroiled in a heated debate about whether it was better to obtain consumer credit card information *before* or *after* a trial period with the product. A few team members were adamant about gathering card information as soon as possible, going so far as to state, "*Everyone knows it's better to get the card upfront!*" (in order to automatically process a payment at the end of the trial period). However, other team members were completely opposed to this idea.

When our discussion reached an impasse, we agreed to compile data to support our divergent approaches and present our findings at the next team meeting. Employing the true scientific method, our most enthusiastic supporter of taking the credit card information first presented research that actually disproved part of her hypothesis. She'd found that, as expected, potential clients were less likely to convert to paying customers when they *weren't* asked for the payment details up front. However, her research also yielded the finding that the wait-for-payment-info method significantly increased customer loyalty. Defined as the length of time consumers continued using the product after just one year, greater customer loyalty would ultimately lead to higher profits, even with lower initial conversion rates.

When she saw the long term potential, her resistance vanished, and the team was able to move forward with great success. Had she leaned into confirmation bias instead of employing the full scientific method, the team would have remained in conflict, and the best long-term choice might have been ignored.

When it comes to making decisions and implementing new ideas, you can see how the practice of challenging your preconceived notions can lead to some mind-blowing discoveries. Applying the true scientific method is a sure-fire, proven way to shift your mindset, be your own boss (at least inside your head), and take advantage of the many opportunities in front of you.

BUNNY

You hit the nail on the head, Chris: There are always opportunities right in front of us, even if we can't see them because we're stuck viewing things through an old, fixed lens. Understanding confirmation bias and applying the scientific method to counter it is one way to change your perspective, but with my background as a therapist, I want to take a minute to talk a little more about *mindset*.

Your ability to shift your mindset is one of the greatest tools you have in creating an intentional life. Even when you feel like you're stuck in a painful situation over which you have no control, everything can change in an instant if you shift your mindset.

For example, if you're an employee, and you believe you don't have control over what you work on or what your life looks like (known as *fixed* mindset), it is extremely likely you will somehow, probably unconsciously, give up your own inherent power to improve yourself and your life. Maybe you'll tell yourself you can't stand up for yourself because if you do, you'll lose your job. You might close yourself off from new ideas or education that could massively level up your life. Though opportunities may be right in front of you, you won't be able to see them if they do not fit with the picture in your mind.

But if you shift your perspective, choose to view your employer as your partner, believe you do good work for a good reason, and decide you have control over your choices and reactions, you will have moved into a *growth* mindset—and your entire professional experience will change. I guarantee it.

With a little inner work, those painful circumstances you've been facing no longer have to plague you. When you focus on what *can* change instead of what you think *can't*, and you start to seek out opportunity, things look different almost immediately. Life feels better. Whatever you're experiencing becomes more enjoyable.

A growth-based mindset is also one of the key qualities of a good boss. Because bosses are in positions of influence, they have the power to inspire changes in themselves and others. Doing so in a positive way begins with mindset. So, now that you're working remotely, thinking like a work-from-home boss is your next step.

In your recent remote work experience, if you've been focused on resentment, fear, uncertainty, or resistance, you're not alone. And, now's the time to make a change. Working remotely is a phenomenal opportunity in so many ways, so why not enjoy it? Shifting your headspace to be more positive and open to opportunity *will* improve your experience.

I know because I've had plenty of practice. As an entrepreneur, I've been my own boss for years. For much of that time, I've worked at home. I've learned that being your own boss, as exciting as it is, can also be scary. There are clear moments when I'm on top of the world: when I'm sharing my story on stage, seeing a client's eyes light up as they finally grasp a pivotal concept, or watching a team transform while I hold space for them. Those are the high moments, the ones that make entrepreneurship worth it.

But there are also low moments, times I've questioned my own choices, doubted my decisions, and wondered whether I'm actually helping my clients solve their problems. Every time I find myself in that negative mental place, I know it's a mindset issue. Somewhere, somehow, I have convinced myself of a truth that is not actually true.

Case in point: Early in my entrepreneurial journey, I used to spend more hours than I will ever admit staring at my bank account balance, willing it to be higher. I would beat myself to a pulp over the fact that even though I put consistent energy and effort into my business, it wasn't producing a steady paycheck for me. I wasn't getting what I expected, so I was convinced I was doing something wrong.

But the real problem wasn't the bank balance. It was *me*. I believed I deserved a steady paycheck for the energy and consistent effort I'd invested in my business; since that wasn't the case, I concluded I was to blame—even though steady paychecks are almost never how entrepreneurship works! I spent oodles of time blaming myself for not doing things that maybe I should have done, or for doing things I shouldn't have, or for not taking action fast enough or too fast or whatever. I got all caught up in my head over these things, even though no one else aside from me knew or even cared whether I was doing those things at all. I was viewing things through an unproductive lens, and my mindset was in serious need of adjustment.

Fortunately, thanks to my therapist background, I saw what was happening. I was able to let go of the belief that predictable pay was part of entrepreneurship. I embraced a new perspective, one that measured success based on consistent, productive activity, not just the contents of my bank account.

I'd love to tell you that was the last time my mindset needed adjusting, but that would be a lie. The truth is, having a positive outlook is much more of a practice than a destination. As life throws its curve balls, our resolve is repeatedly tested. With each new hurdle or obstacle, we choose how we will process it. Will we view things through the old lens? Is doing so positive and productive? Or will a mindset shift help you make the most of your current situation?

Over the years, I've learned there are a few super-solid ways I can make sure my thoughts are where I want them. To illustrate, I'll share an example of a challenge I experienced and how these tactics helped me stay positive and true to myself and make the most of it.

The situation: A new business of mine failed, just one month after its grand opening. I wish I could tell you this was a first for me, but it wasn't my first business failure, and I can almost promise you it will not be my last. Still, when it happened, I'll admit I got hung up in my head.

Beating yourself up over your own mistakes or failures is part of the human condition ...but we don't have to wallow in it. I want to share how I embraced it in the hopes it will make your head a more positive place and guide you smoothly through your next (or past) challenge.

1. Always allow core values to guide you.

Normally, when I am struck with an experience or thought that will benefit my community, I'm quickly motivated to take quick action to deliver it to as many people as possible, even if it paints me in a less-than-perfect light. I'm willing to put myself out there because I believe deeply in authenticity. However, I almost didn't share this business failure with my colleagues and connections. For a moment, I thought about keeping it to myself.

Though it's easy to share business growth tips and client wins, writing about an intimate, recent failure is a raw process. Being *that* authentic with my network, especially my most valued business partners and clients, meant I'd likely receive some judgement for putting it all out there. But I finally decided that no matter how painful some of those comments might be, sharing my experience felt right and authentic. So I went for it.

In the end, my business failure turned out to be a powerful reminder and opportunity to recommit to my core values by choosing to be transparent and honest. But it took making a conscious choice to focus on my values, not my fears, for me to get there.

2. Remember that "failure" can actually lead to success.

In navigating this business failure, I was initially terrified that my clients and prospects would look at me and wonder, "What kind of business coach can't make a business successful? Why would I hire someone whose last venture failed?"

Amazingly, as I shared my decision with my community, the opposite happened. Rather than judging me for my failure, numerous clients and friends told me they were proud of me. They respected me more for recognizing the situation was not aligned with who I am and my values. Making the choice to accept my failure and announce it publically actually led to several new clients and strengthened my network of connections, too.

3. There are always lessons to learn.

One of my coaches told me once, "Some businesses fail because of you, but some businesses fail in spite of you." Could I have done things differently with the hand I was dealt in this particular business situation? Maybe… and maybe not. Sometimes I still need to learn my lessons the hard way. I used to fight it, but over time, I've learned to accept this pattern and process. I even lean into it now, knowing my personal experience makes me a more valuable coach and consultant. Each and every business I currently own, as well as those I have owned, sold, or closed in the past, has provided a plethora of personal and professional lessons. Because of what my experiences have taught me, everyone I interact with benefits.

So, when my business failed, rather than blaming myself or wallowing in what ifs, I took a close look at what had happened. This lesson had cost me financially; what had my investment taught me? I quickly realized I'd held on too long, trying to make the venture work because the concept was close to my heart. Looking back, I could see there had been writing on the wall long before the end had finally come. Had I recognized the signs earlier, I could have folded, taken the rest of my cash, and reinvested in my vision in a more strategic way. Lesson learned for next time.

4. The end is really the beginning.

Yes, my business failed, and yes, it was a painful experience. However, my mindset about it is strong and positive. I actually feel grateful for the experience now that it is over. Here's why.

Before the business even launched, people I trusted waved red flags that this model wasn't a fit with my very intentional lifestyle and time management choices (for example, it required a brick-and-mortar building and my frequent presence on-site). But I chose to focus on my passion for the project instead of heeding their warnings. I justified everyone's skepticism by assuming they did not understand the business model well enough.

I'm humble enough to admit I was wrong. They *did* understand, more than I did. And while I still believe in the business concept overall, I can now see it was the wrong business model for me.

However, I don't feel badly about my choices. In fact, my intentional mindset choices allow me to view this failure as an opportunity to do something new and better. Because of my failure, I've learned a ton, my other businesses have grown, and I've met amazing people. I know wherever I go next, I'll be even stronger because of my experience.

Your failures can help you reach new heights, too, when your head is in the right place. With a positive mindset, it's easy to see failures for what they really are: natural precursors to exciting, new opportunities.

If you're ready to change old, unproductive thought patterns and move from a fixed mindset to one focused on growth, this is your moment. You now have two proven approaches. You can:

1. Apply the scientific method as Chris suggested, busting through your bias and reframing your perspective to think like a boss.

2. Intentionally view your past perceived failures through the lens of positivity. Look for lessons learned, gains, and unexpected opportunities to help shift your mindset.

Both avenues will help you step into a positive headspace that is consciously aligned with your values and goals. There, you will discover your true "boss mind."

TAKE ACTION!

Confirm Your Bias *(Chris)*

Choose a real challenge you are working through right now. It could be work-related or life-related. Write out the assumptions you are firmly holding onto in this situation (the things you *know* you are right about).

Then, challenge your thinking. Look for evidence to *discredit* those assumptions.

Tip: Really do your homework. Rely on research and data. Also, keep track of when you sense your personal beliefs and emotions are trying to steer the results of your findings.

Allowing Failure to Be Your Greatest Teacher *(Chris & Bunny)*

Choose a scenario from your past where you feel you failed (in your life or career).

Then ask yourself the following questions:

1. How can I reframe this event in my mind so I see it as a point of personal growth, not a fixed negative event I can't get past? What major lessons (which will help me grow and move forward) did I glean from this event?

2. What did I do (my contributing actions and behaviors) to facilitate this failure?

3. What aspects of this failure could I have controlled? What was out of my control?

4. If I were put in a similar situation again, how would I navigate it differently, and what would I do similarly?

5. What actions can I take and what mindsets can I adopt to ensure I learn from my *next* failure?

Journal It Out *(Bunny)*

What is one thought or concept you took away from this chapter?

Did any familiar themes, fears, or habits of thought come up for you as you read this chapter? Do any of these patterns have the power to limit your progress? If so, how could you alter your thinking and reframe those thoughts to keep you moving forward?

Right now I am feeling:
_____

A challenge I am currently working through is:
_____

What is one big, past failure would you like to be able to reframe as a time of learning and growth? _____ *(use this answer as your the "Allowing Failure to Be Your Greatest Teacher" exercise)*

CHAPTER 7:

STAYING POSITIVE WHEN THINGS SUCK

BUNNY

Throughout this book, we have offered all kinds of solutions, tactics, and approaches to reclaiming your sanity and your life while working from home. We laid a foundation with values (Chapter 2), discussed the play between acceptance and control (Chapter 3), talked about how to create healthy boundaries even if there's literally not much space in your home (Chapter 4), inundated you with productivity hacks to ensure you get s#!t done (Chapter 5), and emphasized the importance of a positive mindset to help you think like a boss (Chapter 6). It's official: You now have the tools and the space to actually thrive working from home. Hooray!

However, we'd be remiss if we promised you everything would be peachy with these resources alone because there's still the outside world to consider.

It's completely unrealistic to expect you to operate unaffected by external circumstances (you know, everything happening outside your house). So, now that we have our internal environment on lock and know how to be productive and successful in our own little worlds, it's time to talk about how the rest of the world factors in.

Thanks to the prevalence of media (both social and non), things like elections, recessions, riots, and even royal scandals create ripple effects that inevitably infiltrate your little corner of life. When the outside world enters your world, all the tactics we have been teaching you *really* get put to the test.

In those moments, when the outside world rocks your inner world, how do you stay the course? How do you remain positive? What do you do when it's not just *your* day or week that heads into the ditch, but it starts looking like the whole world is headed there?

Not to change gears in the middle of my own story (even though that's totally what I love to do), but a while back there was a huge fight during an NFL game because of inexcusable, unprofessional conduct that occurred with just a few seconds left in the game. After going back and watching it over and over, I realized what actually happened was a series of bad choices, by a lot of individuals, in quick succession, which ultimately led to behavior that could end someone's career.

Afterwards, some people said the player brought it on himself. Others accused the other players and coaches involved. But to me, it looked like a whole lot of subconscious, ingrained reactions… and very little actual, conscious thinking.

If just *one* of those individual players had stopped reacting and instead paused to think, "What is the best choice I can make right now?" that specific chain of events might have never happened.

But stopping to think in the midst of a chaotic and emotionally charged situation is, unfortunately, the opposite of our default response as human beings. Instead, we usually default to reacting habitually based on old, unconscious thought patterns. These knee-jerk reactions can quickly trigger others to react, too, which, as in the case above, can lead to behavior so unprofessional it burns some serious bridges.

Unconscious and reactive thinking can also lead to a rush on toilet paper at every grocery store across the nation. Even when toilet paper has never historically been a thing people hoard en masse.

The inexplicable toilet paper phenomenon that swept the country when the virus began to spread is a perfect example of the powerful influence of the outside world. When the news reports started warning of TP scarcity, what did people do? Instead of stopping to think, "Hey, how much toilet paper will our family really use? Maybe we should just buy that much," they rushed out to the store to buy way more than an entire orphanage could use in five years, much less the next five months.

Is it a good thing to have that much TP in your house? Is it a bad thing? Are the people who bought up all the toilet paper good, or are they bad? Depending where *you* fall on that spectrum, your answer will be different. But really, who's to say who's right and who's wrong?

Rather than judging one another and getting sucked into an endless, unproductive debate, let's take a step back. The stuff that happens in our world isn't inherently good or bad. What happens just happens; it is what it is. Designating something as "bad" or "good" is a choice.

Think about that for a moment. In that split second after something happens, before you do anything, you have two choices: You can react habitually, or you can consciously choose how you want to perceive the thing that just happened.

That may not sound like a lot, but it's a big deal. When you choose *not* to react and instead choose to view the world through your positive mindset, though the world itself may not change, *your experience will.*

When your mindset is positive, and you are looking for good things to happen, you will see the positive in the things that happen to you and around you. When your mindset is negative or reactive, and you believe bad things happen in the world or to you, I guarantee you'll find a way to see the downside of just about every situation. Whichever angle you take, the world will reflect it back to you.

Think that all sounds too woo-woo or dramatic to be your life? I bet it's not. Think back to a time where you experienced some kind of outside influence. Maybe you recall a time you got cut off in traffic. What did you do? You laid on your horn for the next half mile, speeding dangerously just to flip off the other driver and cut them off in return. As you swerved, you likely spilled your coffee on your new shirt, then found yourself cussing and blaming the nearest lifeform (for me, that's normally my husband because I *never* blame the dog), potentially damaging an important relationship out of anger.

All because someone, whose story and circumstances you don't know, made one poor driving decision and cut you off.

Right now, circumstances being what they are, you may be feeling a bit more fearful or negative than you used to. Fortunately, whether you've been viewing your life through a negative lens for years or just a few months, you still have the same golden opportunity. You *can* change your experience, no matter what is going on in the world, by changing your reactive lens to be more positive and conscious.

Choosing the positive is how we can stay positive, even when the world around us is crashing and burning. (Not that any of us has ever experienced that, right?)

CHRIS

I agree, Bunny, that the power to choose is inside us all. But I want to dig a little deeper into this idea of choice in response to what the outside world throws at us because I've personally found it's not always easy to see the positive, even when it's there. When things outside your window are looking bleak, and you desperately need some motivation for your mojo, return to this chapter, and know we've got you covered.

For you, experiencing the influence of the outside world might mean you pick up a call from a friend and receive some sad or unexpected news. Or, you find yourself scrolling through your social media feed and stumble upon yet another political commentary that makes you groan out loud. Perhaps you are running on two hours of sleep because a dear relative is in the hospital, or maybe it's hearing about yet another shooting or riot that puts you over the top.

When tough scenarios like these occur, it can wreak havoc on your emotions and send your perfectly planned day/week/year into a tailspin. You may want to retreat to your bed, pull your shades shut, and bury your head underneath the covers, vowing never to leave again. Staying *positive* during these times, lovely as the concept is, can be a real challenge.

To give you some perspective on your own feelings and reactions to the crazy, insane world out there, I suggest starting with learning the four key human responses to feeling overwhelmed or frustrated.

Studies have shown that when things hit the fan, humans tend to opt for one of four different responses. When that breaking point arrives, the way we react is influenced by two key factors: our perception of the control we have over the situation, and how much we care about the circumstances and the people involved.

According to economist Albert Hirschman and author Adam Grant, who has expanded upon Hirshman's theories, the four actions we may take when we're pushed to the edge are *exiting*, *voicing*, *persisting*, and *neglecting*. To help you figure out which may be happening for you, let's take a closer look at each.

If *exiting* is your go-to tactic, when you sense a situation is completely out of control, you choose to exit the scene. The circumstances are too dire, and your commitment is not strong enough to keep you there any longer. Exit-associated actions include leaving the country because you strongly oppose the policies of an administration, quitting your job because you can't tolerate the way your boss manages you, or leaving a relationship because your spouse is critical and demeaning. In today's world, exiting has become more difficult because so much feels uncertain, and there are fewer physical places to which you can actually *go* without assuming risk.

Voicing is the second key human response, and it happens when you care so deeply about a situation you feel compelled to speak up. By allowing yourself to be seen and heard, you believe you are encouraging positive change. You might demonstrate your opinion by participating in a protest or running for office, opening a conversation with your boss about the kind of support you need, or talking with your spouse about healthy communication.

When you're 100% committed to a flawed situation and have given up trying to change what's not working, it's known as *persistence*, the third key response to frustration. Essentially, you're trying to "stick it out" for the sake of the cause. You might continue to live in a country, pay your taxes and support the government even though you disagree with the policies of elected officials. You might also accept the disrespectful behavior of your boss and still continue to give your absolute best when you're on the job because you care about the company's mission. Or, in today's world, perhaps you always wear a mask in public places where it is requested or required, even if you're not convinced doing so is actually helpful.

The fourth and final response happens when you've resigned yourself to the fact that nothing can be done to improve the situation, you've essentially checked out, and you are only doing the bare minimum to maintain the status quo. You are exhibiting *neglect*. You might avoid all political discussions and abstain from voting, remain in a job you dislike by simply going through the motions; or stay in an unhappy marriage by taking up a hobby that keeps you out of the house and away from your spouse.

As you've probably experienced, the *exit-voice-persist-neglect* model is, in fact, a spectrum. There are shades and overlapping interactions amongst all these responses, and our habits and personal biases sway us. Still, you may be able to identify a go-to pattern or two you tend to use to help you deal with frustrating circumstances. Knowing how you tend to respond to frustrating situations can help you recognize when you're headed towards the danger zone in the future, hopefully in time to avoid disaster.

When you *do* notice yourself heading down that well-worn path, what can you do about it? Already in this chapter, Bunny has given you some great advice on pausing in moments of overwhelm, checking in with yourself, and choosing to intentionally find the positive, rather than just reacting to whatever negative circumstances surround you. As she's shared, in every moment, the power to choose your own reaction is within your grasp, and choosing to focus on the positive will improve your experience, even in negative situations.

But if you're like me, just choosing to see the positive for myself in a situation sometimes feels… not enough. Maybe you, like me, wish you had the power to influence *other people*, not just yourself. If we can shift our mindset to change our own experience, what about creating a better experience for others, too? Can we positively impact *their* experience?

It may sound like a Jedi mind trick, but it turns out you actually *can* influence the experiences of others. There's even real, hard data to support that claim.

Over the years, I have written many articles about improving happiness. The basic formula is to increase the things that positively influence your mood, emotions, and overall state of mind and to limit exposure to toxic people and information. In short, happy people choose to expose themselves to positive input, regularly.

But as I discovered in an article in *SUCCESS Magazine* covering an interview with Michelle Gielan, researcher and author of the book *Broadcasting Happiness*, there is also a proven approach to "infecting" (too soon?) people with the happiness bug.

Given the current state of the world, it seems a timely, if absurd, notion. If one person really can influence others to adopt a more positive outlook, to feel more hopeful, and to communicate in a more upbeat manner… well, maybe we have a chance to change this world for the better after all.

According to Gielan's findings, in addition to monitoring input, it's equally important to monitor *output*, intentionally transmitting positive intentions and messages to others. She describes it as deliberately broadcasting an optimistic message in everything you say and do. This, it turns out, has the power to create a positive ripple effect.

In one experiment, Gielan partnered with Cornell University to study 689,000 Facebook feeds. She inserted emotionally uplifting posts in some of the feeds and pessimistic posts into others to see what would happen. As predicted, a ripple effect occurred in both scenarios: Facebook users re-posted both sets of material with a similar rate of frequency, proving that we possess a basic inclination to broadcast whatever information we're receiving, regardless of its positive or negative nature.

The fact that *all* of our words, both positive and negative, have the power to create a cascading impact is interesting, if not overly surprising (we've all been exposed to enough media to sense this truth). But what about the words we *don't* say?

Gielan's research also explored the non-verbal aspect of communicating one's disposition. Three subjects were placed together in a room and told to do nothing for two minutes. During the time spent in silence, researchers took note of the body language presented by the participants, including facial expression, arm placement, and eye contact. The purpose of the experiment was to discover the effect of the most non-verbally expressive person in the room on the people around them.

The research determined that if the most expressive person in the room folded his arms, or had a slightly irritated look on his face, the rest of the participants felt agitated or uncomfortable. The opposite was also true. If the most expressive person smiled and exhibited an overall pleasant demeanor, the others reported feeling happier and more light-hearted.

As Gielan dug deeper into this phenomenon, she applied her findings to the business world, pointing out that exposure to only three minutes of depressing or disturbing news at the beginning of one's day had a 27% likelihood of negatively affecting emotions and overall mood for up to eight hours. Conversely, she stated, "An optimistic mindset is infectious and lays the groundwork for individual and collective success. Our research shows that broadcasting optimism can increase sales by 37% and can increase the likelihood of a promotion over the next year by 40%."

That's powerful stuff. But it doesn't stop there. For those who aren't content to simply take the passive route of absorbing and broadcasting, who prefer an *active* approach to influencing the mindsets and attitudes of others (me!), Gielan offers up a tool called "The Power Lead." Ultimately, we are not responsible for the emotional states of others, and we cannot be expected to revolutionize the mindset of someone deeply rooted in negativity. However, using The Power Lead, you can effectively shift the mood of most everyone you encounter throughout your day.

Essentially, this tool is about your interactions with others. By making an intentional choice to infuse positivity into every conversation and verbal response you share, this positive spin opens the door for people to search for an upbeat reaction in return. Even if they don't come up with anything specific on the spot, you've planted a seed by sharing a positive tidbit of your own.

For example, when you are the one starting the conversation, rather than using the stock opener of, "How are you doing?" or, "How's your day going?" try leading with something simple and positive in your mutual world: "Wow, what a gorgeous day—perfect weather to take in the fall foliage. How are *you* doing? Do you have plans for the weekend?"

Now, I'm naturally curious, so after reading this article and learning about Gielan's findings, I wanted to give it a whirl on my own. So, for three days, I consciously tweaked my personal broadcast to be more positive. I started with my daughter at the breakfast table. "Wow, what a beautiful morning," I commented. "Aren't these eggs perfect? How great that we can share a meal together as a family today!" Almost as soon as I started shifting my own mood and output, I noticed she became consistently more upbeat. Her positive mood lasted the rest of the morning. I tried it with my neighbor, too, whose baseline attitude tends to be a bit cranky. I started with a flattering comment about her garden before asking how she was doing. She softened up and became warmer within moments of our initial interaction.

In addition to the robust amount of research I found on the topic, my experiment had me convinced. Now there were *two* things I could share to help folks influence their experience: adjust their input (my old standard), and adjust their output, too.

Mind. Blown.

Of course, despite our best efforts, there will always be moments when the negativity of the world tries to seep in. When it does, remember you're far from powerless. If you feel off track, surround yourself with as much positivity as you can possibly find. (And if you're really struggling, know that it's totally acceptable to get some extra help from a coach, counselor, or therapist.) Bottom line, do everything you can to intentionally boost your own headspace, and you'll positively influence not only your own life but the lives and experiences of those around you, too.

Remember, even when the world is full of fear and piled high with uncertainty, there are plenty of successes, victories, and things to celebrate. If you start looking for them, you're guaranteed to find more. Then, you can broadcast that happiness straight out into the world.

TAKE ACTION!

Let's Change Our Minds! *(Chris)*

On a scale of 1-10, with 1 being constantly negative and 10 being obsessed with happiness, typically where do you idle on the spectrum?

What influences (internal or external) could you change to improve that score?

Now, consider the four frustration archetypes: exiting, voicing, persisting, and neglecting. Which tends to be your default response:

- when things really bother you at work?

- when things really bother you at home?

- when things bother you in your local community?

- when things bother you in the larger word around you?

- Is there anything you would change about your reactions? Why?

Get Your Happiness On *(Chris)*

This week, feed your brain a happy meal by reading, watching, and listening to things that make you laugh, or spending time with someone who makes you smile, at least three times a day. (And limit taking in negative information to a max of 20 minutes a day.)

The Power Lead *(Chris)*

Practice *The Power Lead* at least once a day this week, and see how it impacts other people's moods. Write down the results in your journal.

Journal It Out *(Bunny)*

What is one thought or concept you took away from this chapter?

Did any familiar themes, fears, or habits of thought come up for you as you read this chapter? Do any of these patterns have the power to limit your progress? If so, how could you alter your thinking and reframe those thoughts to keep you moving forward?

Right now I am feeling:

_____

When I feel overwhelmed, I commit to doing this one thing to pause and shift my mindset to be more positive:

_____

CHAPTER 8:

HOW TO MAKE A DIFFERENCE EVERY DAY (SERIOUSLY!)

CHRIS

Jerri, a long-term client of mine, was basically driving herself crazy in her efforts to create strong business goals. She had identified plenty of surface-level improvements she could pursue—things like increasing her social media presence, offering new products and services, and of course, bringing in more money. But after mulling over six of her top picks, she was no closer to settling on anything that felt right to her.

As we talked about it, I mentioned I thought it was curious that Jerri used the phrase "nothing felt right." I asked her to expound on what that meant to her. She shared that over the past five years, she'd been focused on expanding her business because she had hoped by doing so, she'd feel some sense of personal satisfaction in the process. But that hadn't been the case. On the contrary, the business she'd once been so passionate about had become a burden.

A series of back and forth questions ensued. After some deeper exploration of her frustrations, we began to uncover something new: the deep-seated motivation she'd been searching for. As soon as we hit on it, her voice lifted and her enthusiasm came through, and, though she'd been stuck and struggling just a few minutes before, Jerri happily and clearly stated her number one goal: *She wanted to use her unique gifts to make a positive difference in the world.*

No matter who you are or what kind of work you do, I'm guessing Jerri's dream isn't too far from your own.

BUNNY

That's definitely true for me, Chris, so much so that the idea of making the world a better place is incorporated into my business name and clearly stated at the bottom of every single email I send out.

Much like Jerri, making a difference is vitally important to me, and I think a lot of us would agree. We feel called to contribute, to make our mark, to deliver a positive impact during our lives. But it can be hard to know what that even means. Like so many things in our world, making a difference is deeply personal. How you accomplish that goal is as unique as you are. Furthermore, just as you continue to grow and evolve throughout your life, your definition of making a positive difference may shift over time.

For example, if you had asked me when I was in my late teens how I was going to make a positive difference in the world, I might've told you I would study hard and get good grades so I could continue my education. In my twenties, I probably would have referenced the changes in the lives of the children I counseled as a crisis counselor. Once I became an entrepreneur, making a difference grew into positively impacting my clients' lives and businesses and encouraging them to make a difference in their own way. And, as a parent, it means ensuring the children I've brought into this world have a happy and positive life, so they, too, can go about making the world a better place in their own unique ways.

Though these answers are all different, at their respective times, they were all true for me. Likewise, only you can answer for yourself, right now, what it means to make a positive difference in the world. Then comes the hard part: You have to actually get out there and make it happen.

I'm sure Chris has a formula or fancy acronym that will spell out beautifully how you can take specific steps to make the world better, but for me, *making a difference simply starts with authenticity: knowing yourself deeply and being intentionally true to who you are.*

Summed up in just a few words like that, being authentic sounds easy. But in today's world, where engagement happens largely via social media, it's a never-ending competition to produce the most enviable highlight reel. Even though we know these platforms aren't reality, continuous exposure to them messes with us. Not only do they frequently cause us to judge ourselves way too harshly, they encourage inauthenticity. We never see others for who they really are; all we see are the "perfect" parts they're willing to share publicly.

In this surface-deep world, it's hard to truly connect with one other. So when the chance for connection arises, we jump at it. I believe this is why so many of us head over to the "about us" page when we visit a company's website (at least I do!). Before we make our final decision on whether to buy, we want to know who's behind it. For me, seeing the faces of the people with whom I'm investing, reading about what they've accomplished, and knowing my purchase will help them achieve their real-world goals makes me feel good about investing in their service or product. If they openly share what they've overcome in their efforts to be successful, even better. Who doesn't love an underdog story? My point is, a company's willingness to authentically share who they are and what they're doing gives us a way to "buy in" emotionally. Even if we never meet these people, their willingness to share something *real* about themselves brings their product or service to life.

So, if you're looking for more authentic connection in your life (which, if you're hoping to make a difference in the world, you probably are), there's one guaranteed way to make it happen. It's simpler than you think: Start sharing your *real* story.

As much as we look for businesses and teams that are transparent with us as consumers, many of us don't take the same approach in our personal lives. Instead, we play our cards close to our chests, keeping our stories of success and failure to ourselves. We fear judgement and rejection, so we hide ourselves away.

But what if that weren't the case? What if we shared more openly with others instead? Gave them a chance to connect with us genuinely? What would happen then? Yes, we'd risk the possible pain of someone else's judgement—but we'd gain so much more.

I know because I've been there, sharing authentically with strangers I've never even met. I do it willingly and frequently, often from stage. Yes, sometimes it's scary to put myself out there, but I keep doing it because every time I share my story and speak about growing up with a disability… feeling different from my peers… dealing with marital struggles… overcoming infertility… and so many other parts of my personal life, I see hundreds of people nodding their heads in agreement and understanding. I share my story, both highs and lows, because my challenges have made me stronger. They have made me who I am today. They are what allow me to recognize and celebrate my successes.

I also share my story because talking about my experiences inspires others to connect more deeply with me, my business, and my passion for making the world a better place. When I share authentically, they get more out of our connection. As a result, they, too, are more likely to make a difference. It's a win-win all around.

So get out there, and start telling *your* story.

"But Bunny," you may be thinking, "I don't have a stage. My story isn't as exciting as yours. No one is listening to me. How can sharing my story possibly make a difference?"

If that's what's running through your head, let go of it right now.

Do *not* underestimate your story by convincing yourself your challenges are not real or that others won't relate to what you've gone through. You have had real struggles in your life: surviving a challenging upbringing, overcoming cancer, dealing with harassment, facing educational disabilities, feeling alone, sacrificing yourself for others, learning *not* to sacrifice yourself for others, and so much more. Plus there are all the challenges of our new, insane world that you're conquering right now: working from home when you never signed up for it, raising kids who are learning through screens, learning to set boundaries with loved ones and ask for what you need without causing arguments, and figuring out how to be productive in the midst of unending uncertainty.

If these are not legitimate challenges, what are?

Our experiences influence and shape us. They are part of who we are. And, our stories are superfood for real connection. If you are willing to open yourself up, I guarantee you will discover you are not alone—not in your struggles, your successes, or your desire to make a difference in the world. Share your story, connect authentically, and you will discover you have an army of supporters ready to help you make the world a better place.

CHRIS

You know me all too well, Bunny. Of course I have an acronym to help improve authenticity. In fact it's part of how you can make *sure* you are making a difference. To share it with you, I'm going to pick up my Jerri story again. Following our motivation conversation, Jerri decided she wanted to leave her mark on the world by teaching unknown start-up companies how to get on the map through unique social media tactics. It was a natural choice since social media was already a proven skill of hers, and she had developed a local reputation of being quite good. But if she wanted to make a real difference, I told her she needed to make sure she did not settle for *just* being good.

She needed to Be BAD—my acronym for shifts she would have to make to achieve her lofty ambition. Here's what I shared.

Be Better.

One of the best pieces of advice I've ever received was, "Be better, not bitter." This catchy little phrase is a great reminder to let go of the tendency to see the world as unfair, especially when everyone else seems to be getting ahead while you feel stuck in the mud. Instead of focusing on what's going wrong, a great antidote to this affliction is to admire what other people have achieved. Allow yourself to be inspired by it, figure out a way to follow in their footsteps, and *learn* how to match their standard of excellence—or, better yet, surpass it.

Be Bold.

Making a meaningful difference also means being bold. Being bold demands courage. It means pushing yourself out of your comfort zone, on purpose. When I decided I wanted to start my own business, I had to make the bold choice to abandon a comfortable and constant paycheck. It's downright scary to leave yourself with no financial net whatsoever while starting up and running a business from your own home while simultaneously raising a newborn.

I'm not saying you need to do what I did, but choose your own bold endeavor. If it feels scary, you are likely on the right track (although I recommend running some of these bold ideas by your most trusted friends and colleagues who know how to strike a balance between purposeful dreaming outside the box and falling completely off the deep end.)

Remember, there is enormous benefit to be gained with every step you take towards realizing a bold dream. Not only do you experience a surge in self confidence and an expansion in your sense of what is possible in your own life, but your boldness also serves to inspire *others* to take bold actions in their lives, too.

Be Authentic.

In my opinion the word "authentic" gets thrown around a lot these days as a hip way of saying, "keep it real," or, "be true to yourself," which has left its meaning watered down and muddled. To keep from writing an entire three-volume book series on the topic of being authentic, I'll cut to the chase (you'll find Bunny and I actually agree on this one): Being authentic is, first and foremost, figuring out who you really are at your core and being comfortable with it. Once you know and accept yourself in this way, the next step is to place authenticity in the driver's seat of your life, projecting that core essence out into the world through your words and actions.

Being truly authentic at all times requires ongoing, mindful awareness of your values and daily choices. This level of awareness is not something that can be achieved overnight, but you can begin today. If you wish to be authentically generous, for example, you can take one simple action today that feels generous. If you want to bring more authenticity to your professional life, start today by weaving one or two aspects of your core values into your regular business practices.

The more you focus on your values, the easier it becomes to recognize the ways in which they show up in your personal and professional life. As you grow accustomed to this new thought pattern, the less conscious effort it will require. Eventually, interweaving your values into your daily actions will be second nature, and living your life authentically will require minimal effort. It will simply be who you are, inside and out. At that point, authenticity will define how you move through your life, every day.

Be Deliberate.

Being deliberate means doing things with clear purpose and conscious intention. Being deliberate means actually *integrating* the Better-Bolder-Authentic philosophy when you face important decisions. Right now, that might mean a) choosing to try out some of your new productivity strategies, b) figuring out how to get your family on board with your remote work schedule and needs, c) grappling with what to say to a colleague who got the promotion you wanted, d) identifying the most peaceful and effective way to reach consensus on a work project, or e) something completely different that's important and relevant to your life.

Before you make your decision, *deliberately* ask yourself three questions:

- How does this help me to be better?

- How does this help me to be bolder?

- How does this help me to be more authentic?

Asking these questions requires you to stop and think *before* taking action (sound familiar? It should!). Your answers will illuminate which of your options align with your values and which do not. Then, the choice is yours.

BUNNY

This is where things start to get really exciting. Just as Chris talked about broadcasting happiness (Chapter 7), once you start projecting your authenticity out into the world, you'll soon start noticing changes in the people around you, too. You'll likely find the deeper and more genuine *you* are, the more authentic *they* are willing to be, too, and the more meaningful your connections become.

Eventually, much like a domino effect, the impact of your choice to live authentically will spread even farther, reaching beyond the people you know and interact with personally. Because each person you impact directly goes on to impact others, your whole community will benefit from your efforts to put authenticity first.

Remember, it doesn't take a huge network, a massive stage, or big, dramatic action to be authentic. It's far more about making deliberate, values-aligned choices every single day.

To illustrate, I'll leave you with a story. Earlier in this book, I briefly mentioned the tale that inspired me to use a starfish as the logo for my business, A Better Place Consulting. If ever there were a story of the impact of taking consistent, values-aligned action, no matter how small or seemingly insignificant, this is it.

> *Once upon a time, there was an old man who came down to the ocean to do his writing. He had a habit of walking the beach every morning before he began his work. Early one morning, after a big storm had passed, he found the vast beach littered with starfish, as far as the eye could see in both directions.*
>
> *Off in the distance, the old man noticed a small boy approaching. As the boy walked, he paused every so often, seeming to stare out at the waves. As he grew closer, the man could see that each time the boy paused, he bent down to pick up an object, then turned to throw it into the sea.*
>
> *The boy came closer still, and the man called out, "Good morning! May I ask what it is you are doing?"*

The young boy looked up and replied, "I am throwing starfish into the ocean. The tide has washed them up onto the beach, and they can't return to the sea by themselves. When the sun gets high, they will die, unless I throw them back into the water."

Dismayed, the old man said, "But there must be tens of thousands of starfish on this beach! Even if you continue until the sun is high in the sky, I'm afraid you won't really be able to make much of a difference."

Glancing down, the boy picked up yet another starfish and threw it as far as he could into the ocean. Turning back to the old man, he smiled and said, "I made a difference to that one!"

CHRIS

In this book, we've given you a ton of ideas and resources, all of which have built up to this chapter. Now, armed with a toolbox full of tools, the choice is yours. Will you be the old man in Bunny's story, questioning the power of your actions, no matter how small? Or will you be the little boy, actively throwing starfish into the sea with a smile, knowing every action you take makes an impact?

If you tend towards the perspective of the old man, or you've ever been in a dark place where it feels like the walls are closing in and your efforts don't make any difference, I want you to know that *I get it*. And, this final story is for you.

Well before the pandemic, I was stuck in an emotional ditch that lasted over seven years. I was fired from a job I loved and had to take one I wasn't thrilled about. My wife and I were struggling with infertility. I was diagnosed with a slew of health problems. And, to top it off, I was dealt financial setback after setback during a time when the economy was in a huge recession.

Watching my downward spiral, my wife saw how negative and almost toxic I had become. Seeking help, she asked my father what she could do to help. He answered, "Darling, he's always been that way."

With nowhere else to turn, she sat me down and told me what my father had shared. It was bone-jarring to hear. It made me question myself, deeply. Was it true? Had I *always* been *that* kind of person? Either way, I knew I couldn't stay where I was. It wasn't going to be easy, and it wouldn't happen overnight, but things needed to change.

So, I surrounded myself with wise and kind mentors, read countless books, and set out to deliberately blaze a more meaningful path for my life. I felt like I was making progress, but I was never really sure—until one pivotal moment.

One afternoon, I got a surprise call from a client I had worked with two years prior. She updated me on how her life had changed. She was in a new relationship, she loved her job, and she was financially secure for the first time in a decade. Her children were speaking to her again, and she had picked up kayaking as a hobby. As she went on to share even more, I smiled and said, "Good for you! You have worked hard and deserve all those things."

She paused for a long moment. "I appreciate that," she said quietly. "But Chris, the real reason I am calling is to thank *you*. I wanted you to know my life is better for having *you* in it."

She hung up, and I slowly rocked back in my chair, letting her unexpected comment sink in. My heart swelled with pride and gratitude as I realized I was no longer the old man, as I'd feared. I was the little boy, throwing starfish back into the sea.

And I'd made a difference to that one.

Now *you* can make a difference, too. Let's go!
Chris & Bunny

TAKE ACTION!

You (& Everyone Around You) Should Be BAD *(Chris)*

The point of the Be BAD exercise is to make sure you are being Better, Bolder and more Authentic, but being Deliberate is where the rubber meets the road. To really make a difference, you must make an intentional effort every day to do so.

However, aiming to accomplish it all every day can be a little overwhelming. Instead, try adopting Better, Bolder, or Authentic as a weekly theme and find a way to be *Deliberate* about its execution. For example, this week the theme is Bold, so you will find a way to be bold at least once a day. Examples might be doing one thing you've never done before, doing something that scares you a little, or having a difficult conversation. Whatever you do, keep a record of what you did in your journal each day.

The next week, choose a new theme. This time, you might focus on being Better, and your daily activity might be reading a book on emotional intelligence, enrolling in a continuing education class, or learning about meditation. Just aim for one thing each day, and keep a record of it.

If you're focused on being Authentic, find unique ways to let the real you out, maybe by sharing a funny picture of you wrangling your kids or singing happily in the shower even though you know you're off-key.

Keep up your efforts for at least a month. If swapping themes once a week doesn't float your boat, try your own approach! Mix and match, or be spontaneous about which of the Be BAD approaches you use. The most important thing is to record what you did at the end of the day in your journal. Record-keeping ensures you are being Deliberate.

BONUS: Getting in the habit of making a difference can be fun and life-changing, so why keep it all to yourself? Share what you have learned with friends, family, and coworkers, or even give them a copy of this book! Let them know you are using the Be BAD philosophy, and encourage them to be Better, Bolder and more Authentic, too. Don't be pushy… just deliberate!

Projecting the Real You *(Bunny)*

To help myself answer the question "What does it mean to me to make a difference in the world right now?" here are a few questions I like to ask myself:

- What did I find most fulfilling in the last six months?

- What do I want to accomplish in the next six months to leave a legacy?

- What are two things I can do today that will positively impact the future?

Answering these questions helps me figure out what actions I want to be taking. They provide a tangible way to know I am making a difference.

To help me stay in this positive, focused headspace, I keep a journal by my bed. Each morning, I start my day by writing down three things I am grateful for. Additionally, from the last question above, I also write down two things I can do *today* to positively impact the future.

At the end of each day, I revisit my list, specifically looking at those two things I committed to doing that day. If I've accomplished them, I enjoy checking them off. If I did not accomplish them, I evaluate those two things in the greater context of the other two questions. Sometimes I discover I did not prioritize appropriately to fit them in. If that's the case, I look at my calendar for the next day and immediately shift a few other things around to make room for my true "make a difference" priorities. Other times, I realize I committed to accomplishing things that weren't actually in alignment and am able to let them go. Either way, the insight I gain from this daily activity is incredibly valuable. I'm confident the same will be true for you, too!

Journal It Out *(Bunny)*

What is one thought or concept you took away from this chapter?

Did any familiar themes, fears, or habits of thought come up for you as you read this chapter? Do any of these patterns have the power to limit your progress? If so, how could you alter your thinking and reframe those thoughts to keep you moving forward?

Right now I am feeling:

_____

With all you know, all your tools, and all the work you've done over the course of this book, *on a scale from 1-10, how confident are you in your ability to be productive while working remotely?*

On a scale from 1-10, how confident are you in your ability to make a difference? What is one thing you can do to help improve your confidence?

CHAPTER 9:

NOW IT'S YOUR TURN…

ERIN (EDITOR)

Chris felt strongly that we needed nine chapters. Bunny thought eight was plenty and refused to write more. Ever the mediator, I insisted we reach a compromise. So, you get a "blank" ninth chapter.

Really, though, this chapter is not blank. This chapter is full of opportunity—and that's not just a funny way of saying some of us didn't want to write any more.

From this point forward, the story is no longer ours. It's yours. So, you tell us. How does this chapter start for you, and where does it end? Now that you have the power to work remotely *and* you know how to make a difference, what will you do next?

TAKE ACTION!

Break It Down *(Chris, Bunny, Erin)*

In case you'd like a gentle shove in the right direction, here's a start. Write out your objectives below, and identify what you'll need in order to reach your goal. Then, keep track of your progress (and setbacks!) in your journal.

Over the next three months I want to…

In order to accomplish this, I need…

This month I want to…

In order to accomplish this, I need…

This week I want to…

In order to accomplish this, I need…

Don't forget to enlist the help of your friends, colleagues, bosses, and family members to keep you going in the right direction!

EPILOGUE
(IS IT REALLY OVER?)

ERIN

Congrats! You made it to the end! And by that I of course mean the end of the book… the end of the old way of living and working… and the end of the era of separation between work and life.

Ready or not, the new is here to stay. Do you feel ready?

If not, that's okay. Don't beat yourself up over it. Just remember that sometimes we have to choose to move forward in new, scary, and exciting ways, even when we don't feel quite ready. The good news is that the more you step out of your comfort zone, the larger and more comfortable your comfort zone becomes.

It's kind of like moving into a bigger house without having to pack up and move all your stuff. How awesome is that?

As you enter the next phase of your choosing, expand your comfort zone, ramp up your productivity, and settle into being a remote work pro, remember that when the going gets tough, you can always come back to these pages.

On all the days in between, when you don't need this book because you're rocking it out like the badass you totally are, just know that we're all still over here, cheering our heads off for you.

Life may not be predictable or easy, but there's no question you have what it takes to succeed.

QUICK REFERENCE GUIDE

Chapter 1 – What Just Happened?

- Acknowledge the trauma recently inflicted on your "normal" life

- Allow yourself to grieve losses

- Learn how moving forward begins with appreciating what you have now

Recommended Exercise(s)

- Shift Your Perspectives

Chapter 2 – What Matters Most?

- Identify and clarify your core values

- Understand the "what" and "why" behind your important choices

- Explore how your "what" + "why" + core values reveal your purpose

Recommended Exercise(s)

- Know Your Values

- The Power of Purpose

Chapter 3 – You Are Where You Are

- Embrace the power of being present

- Identify actions you can take *now* to improve your situation and move forward

Recommended Exercise(s)

- Curb Distraction with the W.I.L.S.S.N. Method

Chapter 4 – Fall in Love with Boundaries

- Prevent overextension and burnout

- Get your life back by creating clear, intentional boundaries

- Learn about the power of saying "no" and how to do it

Recommended Exercise(s)

- Should I "Yes," or Should I "No?"

- Get Yourself Some Orange

Chapter 5 – Insane Productivity

- Get clear on your compelling reason for wanting to be more productive

- Learn 20 ways to rock your productivity

  - *Reduce & Remove*

- *Hone Your Focus*
- *Be Present*
- *Productivity Hacks for Parents*
- Use calendar and scheduling hacks to encourage change

<u>Recommended Exercise(s)</u>
- Just Do It

Chapter 6 – Think Like a Boss

- Shift your mental processes to be more comprehensive and resemble those of a thoughtful and ever-evolving boss
- Combat confirmation bias with the true scientific method
- Understand how failure actually moves you forward

<u>Recommended Exercise(s)</u>
- Confirm Your Bias
- Allowing Failure to Be Your Greatest Teacher

Chapter 7 - Staying Positive When Things Suck

- Identify what you can and cannot control when the outside world's negativity creeps in
- Learn the four stress response archetypes: exiting, voicing, persisting, and neglecting

- Be intentionally happy, and successfully share happiness with others using the "Power Lead"

Recommended Exercise(s)

- Let's Change Our Minds

- Get Your Happiness On

- The Power Lead

Chapter 8 – How To Make A Difference (Seriously)

- See the value in bringing the real you forward

- Try the Be BAD Philosophy (Better, Bolder, Authentic and Deliberate) to guide your actions

- Remember that numbers aren't the only measure of impact

- Be confident that your efforts are worthwhile, and know when you are making a difference

Recommended Exercise(s)

- You (& Everyone Around You) Should *Be BAD*

- Projecting the Real You

Chapter 9 – Now It's Your Turn

- This is the end of the book but the beginning of your next chapter

- What will you do next?

<u>Recommended Exercise(s)</u>

- Break It Down - Formulate your action plan for the next 90 days

Learn more about Chris Harris, co-founder of RefuseOrdinary, at RefuseOrdinary.com

Learn more about Bunny Young, owner of A Better Place Consulting, at ABetterPlaceConsulting.com

And, of course, please visit BossOnPurpose.com

www.ingramcontent.com/pod-product-compliance
Lightning Source LLC
Chambersburg PA
CBHW072028110526
44592CB00012B/1432